W9-BRH-348

Before Your Dog Can Eat Your Homework, First You Have to Do It

This Large Print Book carries the
Seal of Approval of N.A.V.H.

BEFORE YOUR DOG CAN EAT YOUR HOMEWORK, FIRST YOU HAVE TO DO IT

LIFE LESSONS FROM A WISE OLD DOG TO A YOUNG BOY

JOHN O'HURLEY

THORNDIKE PRESS

An imprint of Thomson Gale, a part of The Thomson Corporation

Detroit • New York • San Francisco • New Haven, Conn. • Waterville, Maine • London

LIBRARY OF CONGRESS CATALOGING-IN-PUBLICATION DATA

O'Hurley, John.
  Before your dog can eat your homework, first you have to do it: life lessons from a wise old dog to a young boy / by John O'Hurley.
    p. cm.
  ISBN-13: 978-1-4104-0446-6 (large print : alk. paper)
  ISBN-10: 1-4104-0446-3 (large print : alk. paper)
  1. Dogs — United States — Anecdotes. 2. O'Hurley, John. 3. Dog owners — United States — Biography. 4. Human-animal relationships — United States — Anecdotes. 5. Conduct of life — Anecdotes. 6. Large type books. I. Title.
7F426cbc.O34 2008
636.7—dc22   2007041301

Published in 2008 by arrangement with Hudson Street Press, a member of Penguin Group (USA) Inc.

Printed in the United States of America on permanent paper
10 9 8 7 6 5 4 3 2 1

CONTENTS

PREFACE

I didn't write this book. My dog did.

I shuffled around some of the words. I filled in some of the gaps to match my recollection of the truth, and, in doing so, repaired some of the great liberties he freely took with history, I suspect at my expense. I also labored a bit over the intended meaning in each of the scribblings I found on small scraps of white, lined paper over a period of time, lying underneath the blue satin feet of the Big Blue Elephant — a five-foot-tall stuffed animal postured aside the blue velvet rocking chair where my wife and newborn son, William Dylan, spend most of each day and much of the quiet hours of the night locked in the intimate embrace of nursing. If you were to shift your gaze from Madonna and son down to the base of the chair and onto the deep blue rug, you would see my very white, fifteen-and-a-half-year-old Maltese, Scoshi, spying from deep within the folds of an also-white, fluffy, shag blanket, which he has raked into position — never twice the same — with his front paws.

Scoshi seems to feel perfectly camouflaged here for his recent, self-appointed mission to guard the infant feeding post. From his low perch on the floor, he could easily fire off a few barks across the bow at anyone, even me, who might enter little William's all-too-blue room. The quick hail of barking, however, would eventually give way to a fit of sneezing and snorting as his allergies kicked in. The volatile mix of barking and sneezing would then knock him off balance and he'd fall on his rear end. He'd give himself a quick, arthritic shake — his work clearly done — rake the white shag blanket back into position, lie down, and ready himself for the next attack, or possibly a nap.

From this strategic point, however, Scoshi could also keep one eye trained on the Big Blue Elephant as it cast its very broad, very blue shadow over both mother and child, just inches away. While the Big Blue Elephant had been silent and still for the eight weeks since little William first came home from the hospital, apparently its tranquility and its soft, shimmering baby blue fur and black button eyes were fooling no one, least of all Scoshi. He knew that a Big Blue Elephant must clearly be respected for the danger it represents. If the Elephant made one sudden move toward the feeding chair, it would be go-time.

Over the eight weeks of this silent, blue vigil, however, gravity was beginning to take a toll on the Big Blue Elephant, causing it to slump slowly into an almost impossible yoga pose with its trunk buried deep between its fluffy blue legs (no, don't try this). So, one crisp winter afternoon, early in the new year, I picked up the Elephant, readjusted its stuffing, and attempted to return it to regal form.

As I lifted the blue carcass, that's when I found it — a small scrap of white paper under the left foot of the Big Blue Elephant.

I picked up the piece, unfolded it, and read the words, while my mind stood still from wonder. There were just two lines on a torn strip. That was all.

Dear Little Pink Thing,
Who are you?

From the simple substance of the note, the author was abundantly clear to me. And it was equally clear that this note was not meant for me, but for someone else. It was

9

written by Scoshi, and meant for my first-born son, who lay in the arms of my wife, just a few feet away.

I put the note back at first, a bit embarrassed and ill at ease, as though I had just become an uninvited diary reader, peeking at pages that I should not. But as the weeks passed, I went back time and again. I was as curious about the intent as I was the content.

It was not the last note I would find. Over the next several months, more would appear. Some were longer and more developed, the paper unevenly folded. Gradually they became a small stack that lay beneath the Elephant's foot — I always put them back after reading — and they were beginning to upset their already fragile blue ballast.

I'm not sure when it was that the meaning behind the whole litany of messages began to become clear to me in a larger sense. It couldn't have been more than a few weeks after a few more notes made their way under the Big Blue Elephant's foot.

I was certain of this: These were not random notes. They were secret notes. They were the type of notes that would be passed by hand, from schoolboy to schoolboy to schoolgirl on that halcyon day that boys discovered that girls were no longer *icky.* They were crucial notes — the kind quickly scribbled to a loved one and entrusted from soldier to soldier at the point of no return. They were sacred, final notes that old men write to their children, their wives, and their God that sometimes go undelivered.

These were notes on manhood. They were life lessons from a wise old dog to a little boy who would barely know him.

There is a painful paradox in the overwhelming joy of welcoming little William to our family, and that is that he will probably never have a chance to know the little dog who sits below him so loyally like the Keeper of the Gates. At nearly sixteen, Scoshi has the experience of more than a century of dog years mixed with the crusty, deliberate spirit of a drill sergeant. But his little black button eyes are heavy now. He can no longer hear. He moves slowly with a limp. If he stands too long in one place, his legs slide out from under him. He waits quietly and patiently at the foot of the stairs now, hoping that someone will come along and remember to carry him up. Watching life leave slowly is sometimes unbearable.

Of the many dogs that have crossed the path of my life, Scoshi has been my closest companion. Wherever I would go, he would go. We traveled across the country together. We have shared glasses of wine from the tip of my finger. We have fished together some of the simplest and most unyielding waters of the world. He has run and trained with me for marathons. He has walked many beaches with me, at sunrise and sunset, in celebration and in sadness.

Ultimately, these memories will be only mine, though, not shared by my son. William will go on to play fetch with someone else. Another dog will lick his face. It stings me to contemplate that and hurts even worse to put it into words on a page. But I know that it will come to pass.

Perhaps that is why Scoshi wrote this book: to leave a sort of silent legacy behind. Perhaps it is not enough for him to be the constant guard at the foot of the chair — these little notes are Scoshi's synthesis of life, a crude and simple compass for William, for when Scoshi is no longer there to lay at his feet.

Perhaps, too, these notes were meant for me to discover. I find it so strangely coincidental that these brief little epistles were found, of all places, under the foot of the blue beast that was the cause of Scoshi's constant watch. It was as though he knew that I would eventually find them, as though he wanted me to. In much the same way that the criminal mind will unconsciously turn itself in, the contemplative mind will always find a way to communicate its deepest truths. I think Scoshi meant for me to reflect on them with my son. These were lessons for us both to ponder.

In my own defense, however, I would have eventually gotten around to writing something of substance to Will. Scoshi just beat me to it. No doubt the timing was intentional, too. While I have no proof, I suspect that he simply didn't trust my ability to sufficiently convey the lessons of manhood to my firstborn son on my own. I imagine he wanted first crack at it. After all, there lies at the heart of every grown male a deep desire for the chance to explain the world to a little boy.

My uncle Cal explained the world to me when I was a youngster. He took to me, I suspect, because I was the oldest boy on my mother's side of the family. Uncle Cal was actually my mother's great-uncle, but the universal title of *uncle* was a catchall, and only occasionally had to be footnoted.

Uncle Cal was a very bright man who was employed most of his life with the U.S.

Army Corps of Engineers, and he was an outdoorsman — a hunter and a hiker. He was a trim, angular Scotsman marked especially by a long, snappy stride, a rich digest of stories, a bit of a hearing problem, and a kind of slurry, guttural accent that made anything he said pretty much unintelligible.

He would vigorously exercise all four — the stride, the stories, the hearing problem, and the slurry accent — on his frequent walks (he loved to walk), and many of those walks included me. He would walk and talk, while I would try to keep up with him, taking two or three steps to his one, and try to figure out what-on-earth language he was speaking. I think we walked pretty much all of New England together, neighborhood by neighborhood, field by field, by the time I was ten. I didn't offer much conversation in return. He never had his hearing aid turned up enough to hear me, anyway.

To his credit, though, Uncle Cal always told tales of importance. They were long adventure stories drawn from all corners of the civilized world and five or six different decades, like the one about building a dam in South America or some watershed project in Egypt. He even helped on the Panama Canal. But Uncle Cal was so long-winded

14

— and so painfully slow to deliver in his unusually heavy accent — that you could lose another model-year on your car while waiting for the point of a story. Anytime I felt him start to plunge into a tale of another past adventure, I would drop my head to watch my toenails grow. Perhaps God protects little boys by giving them a short attention span.

I often imagined him on his hunting trips — walking briskly through the thatched meadows without the benefit of a weapon, and simply felling his prey with a well-chosen epic.

But every story had a point, whether you could understand it or not. His passion for nature always seemed to spill over into the every message and moral. He was an outdoorsman, and his wisdom was skewed a bit toward the agrarian:

After three days, fish and guests stink.
If you hunt two rabbits, you won't get either one.
Men and fish only get into trouble when they open their mouths *(my personal favorite).*

Uncle Cal was colorful if nothing else. Regardless of how little I gleaned from his stories, I know in his heart he wanted to be something of a loving mentor to me, for which I am grateful. He did have some impact. I toss my fish and my guests out regularly. I don't hunt anything except errant golf balls, and those I hunt one at a time. And I do know that I get myself in trouble when I open my mouth. The same cannot be said for fish, however, as the safest place for any fish will always be in the pond where I'm fishing.

Perhaps that is another reason why Scoshi wrote this book. His thoughts seem succinct and to the point. Along with his natural distrust in my ability to handle the subject of manhood, he probably senses in me the resurrected spirit of Uncle Cal, a long-winded Don Quixote and self-ordained poet who can successfully obscure the simplest of truths by buckling you over in boredom.

Ultimately — I will never know why, exactly — he reached out to little William (and to myself, perhaps). I know many things about dogs. I know that their love and their loyalty are blessed with permanence. I know that when they wag their tail, it is connected to their heart. But there are many things I do not know about dogs, not the least of which is what they like to ponder and then write about.

So, if you can believe that you can find new purpose with the birth of a child; if you can believe that the world is full of Big Blue Elephants that sit quietly, seductively, yet ominously nearby, no matter how blue or safe our surroundings; if you can believe that the lessons of life that protect us and inspire us are never really new, that they are learned through dog years of experience and then shared with the young who follow; if you can believe in the love of a little old dog for a little boy who will never really know him? . . .

Then you can believe that I didn't write this book. My dog did.

THE ARRIVAL

Dear Little Pink Thing,

Who are you?

You don't eat our food. We don't get any of yours. You don't take walks with us or sleep in the bed with us. Dad likes to hold you. And you sleep in Mom's arms. Ever since you arrived, everybody wants to meet you.

I watch how Mom and Dad pet you. Mom holds you in her arms while you eat. Dad likes to bounce you. He plays with you like when I was a puppy.

I wonder how long we're keeping you.

You seem to be very important to them. So, whoever you are and as long as you stay, I will sit by this chair? . . . and I will be here for you.

And beware of the Big Blue Elephant.

This was the second note. Scoshi expressed in so few words the surprise, confusion, and anxiety we all felt with the arrival of little William, the Little Pink Thing. *Who are you, indeed.*

Scoshi and Betty never saw this coming. We did, obviously, and, to no one's surprise, my wife was better prepared than I. The instant the front door opened on a late December afternoon and a heavily quilted lump was carried to a freshly blued room upstairs, everything in each of our lives changed.

Life had become fairly predictable until that day. We all rose at the same hour of the morning, usually as the first light crept through the white bedroom shutters. My wife and I would each grab a dog and begin the Love Fest. For fifteen minutes we would rub and snuggle with them both to remind them how much they are loved, and that we begin and end each day as a family.

Life was predictable and yet equally spontaneous. We traveled lightly and often. A couple of dogs, minimal luggage packed lightly, and the world became our oyster. We cracked open that oyster regularly.

It is staggering to realize that when you add just seven pounds, fifteen ounces to the mix of life, everything in the world skids to a stop.

■ ■ ■ ■

Although I didn't know it at the time, I had started to prepare for this epic event at the age of twelve, on a spring night in seventh grade. Earlier that day in school, a Catholic school in downtown Hartford, Connecticut, to be precise, I had raised my hand and asked what I can only remember as The Most Embarrassing Question in the History of the World. In a sudden and decisive moment of personal courage, I had asked our teacher, Sister Marie Noel of the Order of the Sister of Mercy, why it was that an infant had the characteristics of both parents, when, really, the father seemingly had nothing to do with the pregnancy.

I had just asked a nun to explain to me the Facts of Life.

There was a silence in the classroom that lasted only an instant, but it was deafening. So was the roar in the class that followed. In my entire career as an entertainer, I don't remember ever having provided so much laughter to so many as I did that day in seventh grade when I asked a Sister of Mercy to explain the Birds and the Bees. Apparently everybody in the world but me had gotten the memo. All my classmates already knew.

I only remember that depth of all-embracing humiliation one other time in my life: six years earlier, in first grade, on the first day of class. I had to use the school bathroom for the first time, but I wasn't sure of the ground rules. I raised my hand and asked my teacher if it was okay to both pee *and* poop in the bathroom. Thinking back, though, I think the roar of the class in this case was not as much from the substance of my query as the sound of the words "pee" and "poop."

Sister Marie Noel had no satisfactory answer for me that fateful day in seventh grade. I think I stunned her with my question, and if she had mustered up any kind of response I wouldn't have heard it anyway. I was too busy trying to crawl inside my school uniform to make myself invisible.

I took the bus home from school that afternoon, a bit bruised but still curious. I decided to lay this dilemma out in front of my father. After all, he was an Ear, Nose and Throat doctor, and while the cavities of his expertise didn't particularly line up with the area of my concern, I thought perhaps he could shed some light on this mystery. I waited until dinnertime to ask once again.

Why does a baby look like both parents?

My father's eyes went dead, my mother gagged, my older sister howled, my younger brothers stopped playing with their food, and we all waited for someone to respond. Apparently, I hadn't learned anything from the earlier episode in the classroom about the volatility of this question.

Your father will talk to you later.

And he did. We sat for hours in the living room that night. My father sat in the deep green, high-backed chair and I sat in front of him in a black rocker. Together we became a Norman Rockwell painting. By dim light at midnight that night, he had forever replaced the Myth of the Stork and Babies-Come-From-God with the harsher and deeper reality of eggs and sperm and fertilization. Finally, and for the first time, I knew what everybody else in the world knew. I knew how babies are made.

It just took me another forty years to pull the trigger.

The pistol was fired on a cold, rainy March afternoon in New York City. I was in New York on Broadway in the musical *Chicago.* By day I was writing my first book, *It's Okay to Miss the Bed on the First Jump.* I was feverishly trying to meet the publisher's deadline, which kept me glued to our bed with my laptop. The combination of the show and the book left me pretty much incommunicado.

So when my wife emerged from the bathroom in our Manhattan apartment on that soupy gray afternoon, she had to make several attempts to rouse my attention.

John . . .

John?

JOHN!

I finally looked up over my reading glasses and arched my eyebrows to see my wife standing still and framed by the door. On her face was the most unsettling look I had ever seen on her. Her eyes were watering, and her voice was tiny and quivered as it carefully spoke.

. . . We're pregnant.

Now, anyway you look at it, this is a defining moment for a man, especially the first time he hears those words, *We're pregnant.* As Abraham Lincoln once suggested, history will not remember what *they* said, but how *we* reacted. In that singular, precious moment when she stood there and so innocently and vulnerably announced the next and most important chapter of our lives, I responded with the only joke that crossed my mind.

Are you sure it's yours?

She turned slowly back into the bathroom and shut the door. But not before giving me a look that told me she clearly realized at that moment that she had married a boob.

The poor attempt at humor aside, we were both stunned by the realization that our simple, self-directed lives were about to change forever.

Little William, the process of your arrival was something of an immaculate journey. Clean and unencumbered. Your mother was never sick or even nauseous. For nine months she simply glowed with your presence. She read every book she could find on maternity and motherhood. She mulled over each Polaroid of every ultrasound reading like it was the proof sheet for your graduation photo. She spent the better part of two months turning a guest room into the Very, Very, Very Blue Room. She chose your clothing and bedding as carefully as she had chosen her wedding dress two years earlier. She embraced parenthood deeply and completely.

I, however, continued to be a boob for the better part of the pregnancy. For me, as for most men, pregnancy is as detached and conceptual as it is physical and real to women. Women's bodies change shape and size as the spirit of new life fully involves them. Their hormones swirl and their moods swing. Their minds move naturally toward their nesting instinct. The couple of calories that I burned at conception were pretty much my last physical contribution to the blessed event. (Although I did try to supplant my inadequacies with frequent hugs and back rubs.)

For men, the experience is like waiting for the subway. We stand in the dark, in a sort of emotional limbo. We know that somewhere down the line a train is coming. We know approximately when, although it could be late. (We also know a subway is never early, so the analogy falls apart a bit here.) But men don't think much about the circumstances of the arrival. A man's mind is set on where the train will take him and the circumstances beyond. We don't typically dwell on the condition of the track, the availability of power, or the curtains in the ticket booth. Most especially we don't give any regard to the fact that the train is growing by the minute and when the train finally arrives, it's coming out from between our legs.

We did attend the requisite birthing class, which we were lucky enough to have in the privacy of our home. I remember watching

26

a video of two actual births. As real and gritty as each delivery was, I wiped tears from my eyes when I saw each child emerge. I wondered how I would feel watching the birth of my son.

So it was nine months of intellectual exercise for me, while my wife did all the heavy lifting. My body and mind stayed essentially intact, except for a few extra pounds from "sympathy desserts."

What changes everything for a man is the presence of pain. Especially when it is your wife's pain. Pain is something men understand. Pain is something tangible and immediate. Pain is when the subway train breaks down in front of you. Pain can be fixed or eased. Men are good at this.

The first pain was in late November, a week before the delivery. Lisa was visiting me on the set of *Family Feud,* the game show that I host. Suddenly and unannounced, she left the set after the lunch break and went home. I didn't know why until I arrived home that evening.

All the lights were low when I came through the front door. There wasn't a sound as I entered. Betty didn't greet me with the tinkling of her collar as she would always do. Scoshi didn't give a preemptive bark at the vibration of the front door closing.

Instead, there was a sitting vigil in the living room. Lisa was lying on the sofa, Scoshi shrouding her head and Betty lying at her feet. Lisa could barely speak, and my heart sank because I knew she was in pain. She had stabbing cramps and was sweating. She was also sick to her stomach. We were a week before the due date, but the cramping was getting more severe. All I could think of was everything that I had not done. My hospital bag was not packed. The video and the still cameras were nowhere to be found. The list of must-call phone numbers of friends was not at hand. I didn't even have the doctor's number. When I found it I called without knowing what to say. So I gave a rather detailed account of my wife's symptoms to the woman on the other end of the phone, who turned out to be the answering service operator. She knew less about birthin' babies than I did.

Lisa did not give birth that night. She did have a rather severe reaction to the Mexican food served for lunch on the set, which to her memory provided a wonderful warm-up to what would follow a week to the day later.

The call-to-arms contractions began shortly after midnight on Tuesday. My wife endured each one like the saint she is without disturbing my sleep. After all, why wake a sleeping boob?

But by dawn when I awoke she was clearly beginning the process of dilation. Little William was knockin' on Mama's door in ten-minute intervals. I drove her to the doctor's office with the car packed for what looked like a seven- to ten-month hospital stay or a trip at least halfway around the world.

The doctor held her at bay for a while, saying that the contractions were coming at healthy intervals, but that she had not dilated enough to justify admission to the hospital. He recommended that we walk around the block for forty-five minutes to let gravity continue to work its course, and then return for another exam. Once outside I countered with another idea. I suggested that rather than endure a possibly painful walk, we sit at the outside patio restaurant of the hotel next door. And so we did.

In what will eventually rank as one of the most insensitive moments in the history of male/female relationships, I sat there in the late-morning sun enjoying chicken crepes and a mimosa, while my dear wife sat opposite me with a glass of ice water, buckling over in fervid agony in concrete, five-minute intervals, leaving the surrounding patrons gawking and wondering what the hell she had ordered.

The doctor admitted her after lunch.

Waiting for an infant to be born has the uncertainty of a game of keno. The child-in-wait holds all the cards. He is like the multimillion-dollar casino armed with a multimillion-dollar computer. You have a piece of paper and a crayon. *Now we're going to play a game called "I'm Thinking of a Number." You go first.* The game, like their birth, is always in their favor.

It's also about as interesting as keno. Once Lisa was given her epidural (which she still describes as the only tangible proof that God exists) we began the tedious lingering. We talked. We watched television. We played cards. We read. We sat in silence. I finally started to entertain myself by reading the logos on each piece of medical equipment in the room. The time moved like a taffy pull.

There was not a moment, however, that wasn't filled with both the realization and the sense of awe that we would leave the hospital differently than we arrived, that no single moment would so alter the course of our lives together as the one that lay in wait. We came as a couple, we would go home as a family, and life as we knew it would never be the same.

But it's true that the moments that are the most real and the most meaningful are often the quietest. Little William's birth was just that. It was undisturbed by incident, with the possible exception of the fact that I was called to duty at the final, pivotal moment. I had planned to position myself safely out of harm's view by standing where other boobs would stand — up by the wife's head so my first sight would be a hygienic one.

The doctor had other plans for me. He asked me to support one of her feet to give her something to push against to ease the delivery. So there I stood, aiding and abetting in full view of the meaningful and memorable moment of my life.

When the head began to emerge, it was the size of a small coconut. It came to a bit of a point, which made the shape unrecognizable at first. Only after the doctor carefully coaxed the shape forward did the image of a tiny human form appear.

I suppose I have been wondering since the age of twelve, since that wonderfully enlightening night ages ago, how I would react to the moment when my first child came into the world. I imagined theme music, some tears, a moving but terse statement that would send quotation collectors scurrying. I imagined some apocalyptic pose that would be caught by camera for posterity to remember. I imagined very good lighting.

My first thought? *This can't be my child. My wife has mated with a prune.*

He was purple and swollen from his twenty-four-hour, twelve-inch journey. He was also crying, I suspect from the embarrassment of being the only one naked in the room. And he was all hands. The biggest, purplest hands I had ever seen, seven pounds and fifteen ounces of them. I put my finger inside his hand, and his large purple fingers squeezed my finger like a vice. It was the grip strength that a father would give the handshake of his daughter's first date. *This could not be part of my gene pool.* I searched his little purple body for any sign that he was mine. And then he furled his brow tightly, so tightly that the eyebrows almost touched. That was it. The sign I was seeking, the cinched brow. Less than five minutes old and already he had issues. Perhaps he was cold, perhaps he was afraid, perhaps the lighting was not to his liking. No matter. Something was wrong with the world and he knotted his brow to let us know. *He was definitely my son.*

Two days later we brought him home. Two little faces were pressed against the iron-

and-glass door as we arrived. Betty and Scoshi were yelping as we walked up the stairs. As we crossed the threshold everything went strangely quiet. They sniffed the air as they darted around the foyer in silent frenzy, sensing the presence of a new and foreign energy. The Little Pink Thing was finally home.

It wasn't until later that night, after the bags were unpacked, the requisite phone calls made, and the new parents' nerves quieted, that the formal introductions were made. Betty was first. She is our stray mix — a delightful combination of a black Labrador retriever and a dachshund, which has left her looking like an eternal black Lab puppy with all the sweetness of a dog grateful for being rescued. She gave Will a few quick sniffs, but was careful to not acknowledge him with eye contact or lend any importance to the first meeting. She then grabbed one of his tiny red socks that had fallen to the floor and ran down the hall. Clearly this was a cry for help. After that moment she would cry anytime my wife or I went near the Little Pink Thing. She would wedge herself in between us and William anytime we approached. In her little black eyes I could see the same fear of abandonment that I sensed years ago when she was rescued.

It wasn't until one morning months later that she recognized his presence. We were all lying in bed, the dogs and the three of us. William was sitting up, his head still bobbing a bit to and fro from its sheer weight. He reached out with one of his newly discovered and still-oversized hands (complete with opposable thumbs) and grabbed one of Betty's ears. Before we could reach out to separate the two, Betty turned her head sharply to him. In a moment that seemed frozen in time, she leaned out and licked his other hand. She licked it for several seconds while Will's eyes glowed with this new sensation.

Betty still yelps when attention turns toward the Little Pink Thing. I expect this will continue for some time. But one day little William will develop an embrace; he will learn to pet and snuggle. He will be a source of chewies and food dropped from a high chair. He will learn to throw a ball and the Fuzzy Bunny, and he'll be there when she retrieves them. He will learn to take steps and then walk, and eventually he will hike. He will walk around ponds, different ponds from when I was a child, but still searching for the same wonders. And Betty will be at his side, as my dog Taffy was at mine then. And Betty will realize that the Little Pink Thing was not a rival for affection, but simply a companion-in-waiting, and someday they will be inseparable. The thought of all of that waters my eyes and fills my heart.

What Scoshi wrote in his first note was foreshadowed by his introduction to Will. The same night that Betty was introduced, the Little Pink Thing met the Little Old Man, the dog who had been my constant companion for nearly sixteen years. He had been my son at times and my soul mate at others. When I picked him up and put him gently on the really blue bed in William's room, where he was eye level with my son for the first time, he stared at William. He looked up at my wife and me, and then back down at the boy. He continued to stare as if to evaluate the significance of this encounter.

In a gesture that I will remember all of my days, Scoshi inched his arthritic little body forward and licked William on the head. That simple gesture of love was a moment of baptism, a passing of the torch to the Little Pink Thing, as puzzling and enigmatic as he may have seemed. When Scoshi looked in our eyes he saw the love we had for William, and when he looked so deeply in William's eyes, he sensed the importance of the moment.

What resonated so strongly in the first note that Scoshi wrote to William was that he began from the point of innocence and wonder — *Who are you?* The question is as simple as it is profound.

I have come to realize in my oh-so-brief span of fatherhood that *Who are you?* is a question that I will ask continually throughout William's life, and one to which I will never have an answer — never completely, at least. I can say, *He is my son,* but, while true, that satisfies only my deep-seated need to sense accomplishment and authority. It is not his identity. In truth, I suspect I can never fully know him. I can only understand and appreciate what he reveals. My son is my responsibility, but not my property; he is his own little being. To love him and care for him as deeply as I can, I need to respect that he is *other* and not *mine.*

This important distinction reminds me of the first time I saw a firefly, at the tender age of eight. It was a summer night in the Connecticut woods near home. Like little beacons of light they hovered, almost crawling through the air on the thick August night. I remember being so filled with wonder that I caught one in a little jar. I watched in fascination as it flickered on and off in the reflection of the glass until at one point it stopped and fell to the bottom of the jar, either from boredom or the obvious lack of oxygen. I had tried to possess what wasn't mine. The lesson of that night now rings truer than ever, as I hold my son in my arms and feel the significant weight of fatherhood.

Scoshi ended his note with what I believe to be the essence of manhood. *Whoever you are and as long as you stay . . . I will be here for you.* Men are defined, in my experience, by what we commit to. I have known times when I responded to no other impulse than whim, and they were the loneliest times of my life. I am more complete myself by my commitment to others.

So it is that two old men — Scoshi and I — have found a new purpose to life with the arrival of the Little Pink Thing. For Scoshi, his final days will be spent in quiet guard duty at the feet of the ominous Blue Elephant, teaching little William with little slips of paper the meaning of what it is to be a man. The new arrival has given him a reason to be.

For me, I will quietly learn from them both. I will take Scoshi's little notes, so carefully folded and hidden, and let them inspire within me my vision of fatherhood. Like Will, I am beginning from the point of innocence. I am an infant in the world of fatherhood. But Scoshi's second note has pointed my heart in the right direction. I can only be as good a father as my commitment to the responsibility.

I realize, too, that you didn't ask to be born, William. You will teach me probably more than I can ever give you. I will rediscover the simple wonders of the world through your eyes. I know that I have never felt a more profound sense of innocence as when I hold you in my arms. All I can promise you is that I will be here for you. And, for now, that will have to be enough.

The Fishing Gets Better If You Roll on the Worms

Dear Little Pink Thing,

Dad loves to fish. He takes me with him, so he'll probably take you, too.

Here's a tip to remember always — the fishing is better if you roll on the worms.

I have come to regard fishing as a chance to spar with God. Armed with little more than a pole, some line, and a touch of hope, I splash my way in puddles of different shapes and sizes, perchance to wrestle a fish from His tender grip of nature. It is not a level playing field, at least not in my experience, as I have known only moments of victory and hours and hours of defeat. But for all the times that I have stood knee-deep in the waters of His cathedral, casting my line and my gaze in every direction, I know the peace and the joy of having stared Him straight in the eye.

41

Scoshi, apparently, had a different experience

As much as I perceive fishing as a personal and individual pursuit — one that always takes the shape of the fisherman, much like a fine wine takes the shape of the glass into which it is poured — there is something about sharing the early wonder of fishing with your son that feels like the birthright of every father. Perhaps Scoshi's note is the result of the fact that I didn't have a son earlier in my life; perhaps I have always seen Scoshi in that light because he was often my companion for these sacred moments. I guess you could say that I forced fishing upon Scoshi, the way some children are forced to play the piano, only to hate the piano as adults. Fishing is a passion for me, and passions are not easily imposed.

I began to fish from my earliest memories. As a child I was fascinated by what lay beneath the surface of every body of water that I saw. The celebrated pond of my childhood in Natick, Massachusetts, was the focus of my little life. I would walk and explore the navigable edges of the pond every day after coming home from grade school. It was a living, breathing paradise for a boy, with infinite possibilities. It did not, however, hold any fish.

There were many frogs and turtles along the perimeter of its shallow banks, and I found their capture a source of daily entertainment. But my fishing line, with its little red and white bobber, would lie still on the glassy surface for hours. Occasionally the water would ripple from the last throes of the compelling dance of the worm on the hook below. But the pond was, for all of its promise, completely undisturbed by fish.

My father began to realize my love of fishing when I was just out of my infancy. It was hard to miss. At the age of four I felt that every body of water contained fish. Not just the conventional lakes and rivers that occurred to everyone else, but all the puddles and even the standing water that collected at the low end of our yard after the spring melt. All held fish, I thought, so I would fish them all. I would have dropped a line in the toilet if it had occurred to me.

My equipment was pretty simple. I had a small green rod with a little green bait reel. My outfit was just de rigueur enough to let the world know that I had serious expectations as I dropped my line in the six-inch-deep puddle of rainwater at the end of the driveway.

My father had learned to fish from his father. My grandfather was a man of the outdoors. He did not live long enough to ever take me fishing, but his stories of fly fishing the backwoods of Canada for rainbow trout and landlocked salmon were the legends that lived beyond him. To be a fisherman was a badge of manhood. In our family that badge was passed on from one generation to the next. My father spent summers fishing with my grandfather in Canada and along the banks of the Connecticut River where it fed into Long Island Sound. The fact that a fishing rod fit so easily into my young hands made me perfect progeny, I suspect.

The early fishing trips with my father at the ages of four and five are still so crisp in my mind. He had to balance the demanding hours of a young doctor with his love of fatherhood, so every trip was precious to me. We never traveled very far — just down the road and onto Route 9, where there was a lake on the edge of the main road leading out of Boston. We would park at the gas station on the corner, and a dark-haired man who owned the station would give us a simple wave of luck as we crossed the road to the steep embankment of the lake on the other side.

I'd wait as patiently as I could while my father set up my little green rod and reel.

The red and white bobber, a worm on the hook, and I was ready to go. He would cast the line out thirty or forty feet from shore, hand the rod to me, and I would begin my watch over the bobber as it danced awkwardly on top of the silvery veneer. I remember the smell of the lake. It was rich and alive. I breathed it in deeply because there is no scent quite like it. There I stood vigil on the shore, two little hands on the rod, just waiting and watching.

I had not mastered the art of setting a hook at this age, so my father didn't stand by my side, or fish himself, for that matter. Instead, he climbed back up the bank and stood patiently at the level of the road so he could look out over the lake and watch the bobber for any sign of alert.

Every now and then a fish would cross my path. It would be a sunfish, or small brightly colored panfish with tiny mouths and roundish flat bodies. Not exactly the most dangerous or prized catch, but it was all I could handle. As one would tug on the business end of the line the bobber would disappear into the lake. From atop his perch, my father would scream, "PULL, BEBOY!" (my nickname, don't ask). I would pull with all my might and usually send the fishing line flying back over my head. I would hit my father or, with enough notice, miss him and send the entire line, the bobber, and the worm back out into the steady stream of traffic on Route 9. I'm surprised I didn't send the jaws of the fish along as well.

Eventually, I learned to finesse the rod, and occasionally I would be rewarded with a little sunfish. But even as my skills improved, my father always stood watch at the top of the embankment ready to signal a strike, never alongside me.

Today, nearly a half century later, when the computer so easily enhances memories, I did an Internet search to find a satellite map of that area in Natick as I wrote this. The house is still there; the pond is there but smaller and less imposing. The gas station is gone, but across Route 9 is the embankment where, I will always remember, my father stood and taught me the singular experience of fishing.

As I have grown older and now have you, little William, I realize that it was his post at the top of the bank that allowed me the time alone to have my personal experience. It allowed him to watch me fish and absorb the meaning of the moment. Sometimes you have to step back a bit to gain perspective.

As I grew, I continued to drop lines in barren ponds. When we moved to Connecticut a few years later, I became seduced and abandoned by a stream near our house called Trout Brook, well named except for the word "trout," of which there were none. But I still believed fish were everywhere (I maintained this belief well into my teens), so I would dedicate many hours to that premise. Around that time, for some reason driven mostly by my need to "tinker with things," I had taken a more Huck Finn–like approach to fishing equipment and had fashioned a pole out of a long branch, some string, and a cork bobber. Of the several years I spent sparring with God on Trout Brook, every round went to Him. I still remember the feeling of richness from the outdoors, however, and the great expectation that accompanied each cast as though that wooden pole was still in my hands.

The first time Scoshi joined me fishing he was two years old. I was in Toronto, Canada, for the summer doing the two-character comedy *Same Time, Next Year.* The beautiful summer countryside of Ontario has countless fishing holes. Each one called to me.

One Monday, our day off at the theater, I headed up north out of Toronto toward the

Muskoka Lake region. Scoshi was sitting in the passenger seat next to me unaware of the destination, but happy to be out of the hotel room and going for a ride with Dad.

We arrived in the lake area several hours later. I stopped by a bait shop to get the lay of the land and some worms. They said I should have some luck at a small private spot up the road a few miles. Scoshi was fast asleep, midway through a morning nap, when I pulled off the road to park. I gathered up the gear, the bait, and the dog in my arms and headed down a small path, lightly trampled, toward a good-sized pool beneath the trees and fed by a running stream. I would cast my line into nearly virgin waters while my dog sat quietly in the shade at my feet. It was like a portrait of Fishing Americana, only we were in Canada. I put down the gear, the bait, and the dog so that I could take in the feeling of this extraordinary moment with so much promise. It was broken when Scoshi turned and sprinted back to the car.

I chased after him and found him hiding under the car, shaking like he was chilled to the bone. I gently fished him out from underneath and held him in my arms until he calmed down. Then I started down the path again toward the water's edge. I put him on the ground gently and knelt down next to him, rubbing his neck and his face to let him know that this was a special event for us both. Then he ran back to the car.

This happened two more times before the lightly beaten path began to look like a trough I had dug to the water. I grabbed his leash in a last-ditch attempt to rescue this meaningful moment. I tied him to the shade tree with some slack and began the task of preparing my fishing gear. I cast my line and began to make the best of a complicated beginning.

I caught nothing, but it was a beautiful day. And it was private. We didn't see another human being. Apparently they knew what I didn't. I had managed to find the most idyllic spot in Canada that didn't have any fish.

Scoshi eventually calmed down during our day together. He got thirsty from the heat and managed to drink most of the water out of the fishing hole, then he went back and lay down underneath the tree. I didn't pay much attention to him until an hour or so later when I looked over and realized he had taken the plastic top off the bait container, sifted through the dirt, and had pulled out each of the thick, red earthworms. He had laid them on the ground methodically and had rolled over each one of them. As I stated earlier, the rewards of fishing are peculiar to each angler. For Scoshi the joy of fishing meant pressing the worms.

The day ended as it began. I came without fish, and so it was as we left. I scooped up the gear and the dog, and I left the bait still lying in a strange pattern on the ground. We started our journey back to Toronto as the shadows grew long and golden. I looked over at Scoshi, who was facing me in the passenger seat. I thought about how complete I felt. Even without fish, the experience together was still enough. I looked into his eyes as he was staring at me and saw him give me a deep, relaxed look, perhaps in agreement. Then I realized at that moment, he was peeing the entire volume of the fishing hole onto the front seat. *Thanks, Dad. Thanks for the great day.*

I didn't give up on Scoshi as a fishing companion, however. When we were back in Los Angeles later that fall, I discovered a new passion: surf casting. If fishing in fresh water is sparring, surf casting is war. It is man against an angry sea. Long poles, deep casting, stiff winds, and surf. Heavy artillery for the promise of huge returns. Large fish lie beneath the kelp beds that float in the ocean swells.

Scoshi loves the beach, so I figured this would be a perfect match. He loves to run at the water's edge randomly attacking seagulls with his fluffy little presence. The seagulls, meanwhile, will take to the air and fly just low and slow enough to stay a few feet ahead of him, taunting him with their nonchalance. There are great smells for him everywhere.

On my virgin attempt at surf casting I took Scoshi to a special spot north of Malibu, a cluster of rocks that seems to lean out and kiss each wave. The wind sprays an ocean scent. It's a place that begs for Hemingway and a shot of single malt.

I have a twelve-foot pole, a heavy reel and line to hold the bait in place out beyond the surf line. I use squid as bait. Apparently everyone beneath the waves is a fan of it. It is appealing to anything that passes by. I put Scoshi up against the rocks in a crevice to shield him from the wind. I put him on a towel to make it comfortable for him to lie down. He tousled the towel a bit so he could crawl underneath. Only his little white face appeared. It was a moment that needed theme music, something Irish. Old Man, Little Dog, and the Sea.

It was as good a half hour of fishing as I can ever recall. It would have lasted longer, and it should have lasted longer. But I looked back to check on Scoshi while my line lay a hundred yards out deep in the surf. There next to him, once again, was the cardboard bait box, torn open and empty. Scoshi had eaten all the squid. He stared me down with the same look of content-ment that I had remembered from our previous trip. *Thanks for the calamari lunch, Dad.*

I find it strange, then, that in his letters to you, Will, Scoshi would include the experi-ence of fishing so early in his litany. But I wrote earlier that fishing is an experience that takes the shape of the fisherman. For Scoshi, it included a nap under a tree, a chance to roll on some worms, and a sea-food lunch. But most important, it was a precious chance for us to spend time to-gether, as precious as the time I spent with my father, and he with his. I suspect that's why he recalls it with such importance, and that makes me smile.

For me, it has become less about the fish than it is about casting without expectation of return. As I've grown older, I think I've come to look at life that way: If I cast and hit my mark, I have succeeded. If I smile at someone and it is returned, the world is so much better for that moment. If I attempt something I have never done, the attempt is reward enough. But I must continue to cast a line throughout my life. I cannot control what lies beneath.

Plus, I enjoy the chance to splash around in puddles as much as I did when I was four, and fishing still gives me the chance to do something so silly and so important.

So, William, with Scoshi's encouragement, someday soon you and I will disappear together down a lightly beaten path. The same little hand that grips my finger will hold a pole for the first time. I will bait your hook, cast your line, and break the stillness of the water. I will stand near you and together we will watch and wait for the moment when the bobber disappears. Whether it does or not really doesn't matter, because while we are standing there together, as my father once did with me, we are having the experience of fishing, and the chance together to stare God straight in the eye.

BEFORE YOUR DOG CAN EAT YOUR HOMEWORK, FIRST YOU HAVE TO DO IT

Dear Little Pink Thing,
  Dogs don't eat homework. Understand that clearly. Dogs only eat homework that was never done.

As noble a contention as this is, let me start by clarifying this a bit. While Scoshi has never eaten any homework, he has peed on a pair of my white linen pants and a rather expensive piece of artwork that I absent-mindedly left resting on the floor. He has climbed up on the dining room table from time to time and scavenged the remainder of dinner, which once included a quarter-pound stick of butter. He then jumped down and walked away irreproachably, presumably to find another pair of linen pants and some artwork.

He is also guilty of other peccadilloes, like shredding a script just before an important audition. (I was careful not to blame the dog, lest I be guilty of the timeworn cliché myself.) But, to the point, Scoshi has never actually eaten any homework; for more than fifty years, in fact, my life has been free of *canis devore.*

My first experience with the phenomenon of homework being mysteriously edible was in fourth grade, when one of my classmates, whose name now escapes me, announced to our teacher, Mrs. Pierce, that he couldn't hand in his book report because his dog had eaten it. It was completely gone. Gone as though it never existed. Gone without evidence of what was surely the result of hours of thoughtful insight and analysis.

I never realized that a dog was capable of such mayhem. At the time, we had a black Scottish terrier named Mitzi. It never occurred to me that she might be a homework killer or, worse, that she might be using me only to get to my book reports.

The attack probably happened late in the night, when children are sleeping and homework is most vulnerable. A quick leap off the bed, a half look over the shoulder to confirm the stealth, and his dog voraciously riffled through his book bag, nosing his way carefully past the stack of history and math papers to zero in on that unmistakable scent of fresh book report.

Eating a book report, of course, was the lion's kill, especially in Mrs. Pierce's fourth-grade class. One was due every month, like a tax deposit. To miss one meant enduring something the likes of the Spanish Inquisition. You would have to stand in the middle of the class and explain to your peers why the book report had taken such a low priority in your otherwise exhaustive young life. You could try any excuse you wanted, but Mrs. Pierce was too tough, too practiced. Everyone broke under the weight of her examination. Especially, we learned that day, if you blamed your dog. The humiliation of the experience was like a Scarlet Letter that wouldn't rub off for several days. I know this from having suffered through this practice on more than one occasion.

I never thought to blame Mitzi. Instead, when I missed the due date, I simply took the emotional caning in the Fourth-Grade Circle of Penance by shrugging my shoulders through a half-dozen *I dunno's,* trying to soften Mrs. Pierce's blows by boring her.

I was not a great reader. Reading was a slow and laborious process for me, due, I suspect, to some sort of mild learning disorder that stays with me to this day. Each report meant choosing a book, reading the material, and then carefully assembling a list of likes and dislikes of the work. I can only imagine that somewhere a nervous author stood with his toes curled over the edge of a bridge waiting for word of my fourth-grade review.

What I became was a crammer. I would wait till the last possible hour to begin not only book reports, but any academic project for which I'd had a month to prepare. Never with any degree of success.

I remember that year in fourth grade, one particular history report that I executed in this fashion. I had either chosen or been given Christopher Columbus as my topic of study, and had several weeks to put together a report on the celebrated explorer, mounted on a poster. The entire fourth-grade collection of history reports would be exhibited on the walls throughout the school for all to see and share. I waited until Sunday night, some twelve hours before the assignment was due, to begin crafting my work. Instead of reading and absorbing any substance of Columbus's daring career of exploration, I simply cut out his appropriate pages from our family edition of the *Golden Book Encyclopedia* and pasted them directly onto the poster. I added a few hastily drawn pictures of boats and stenciled the title CHRISTOPHER COLUMBUS across the top of the poster.

Not only did I get a poor grade for my efforts, but I also got exactly what I deserved for my negligence. Several hours after the poster went up on the walls of Bugbee Elementary School, the rumbles of laughter slowly began to gather like an approaching storm. Word spread quickly that you had to see O'Hurley's poster. I had no idea why, or what might be the cause of the stirrings — until school let out and I got to see it. And there for all to see, in bold, red-stenciled letters was my poster report on the eminent world navigator: CHRISTOPHER COLUMBUM.

So, William, I clearly understand what Scoshi meant when he wrote that dogs don't eat homework: When we don't take the time to thoughtfully prepare, we blame others for what is our own laziness. We claim not to have had time, when, ironically, time is all we truly have. What separates one person from another is how we *manage* our time.

I continued the pattern of cramming all through my academic life. It is a source of sadness for me, I guess, mostly for having mishandled the opportunity for a richer education. I did learn some, but through my laziness, I squandered most.

This pattern trickled into other areas of

my life as well. After all, homework in school can be seen as a forecast for how we choose to prepare in life, and how well we will achieve.

In 1971, at the age of sixteen, I was a member of the Worst Rock 'n' Roll Band Ever Assembled. That was not the name of the group. That was the fitting description. Our name was the Whiskey Rebellion, and even that name was hastily chosen and painted on the drumhead the night before the only gig we ever booked. It was for my younger brother's graduation dance from junior high school.

I was the lead guitarist and vocalist. This title was handed out too easily. I was at best a third-rate guitarist who knew the beginnings and the middles of perhaps fifty songs. I took guitar lessons for one year, much to my teacher's regret. His final words to me were, "I'm sure you must have other interests." I was never prepared.

Perhaps I was attracted to the thrill of saying that I was in a rock band. Perhaps that is what made me say yes to the junior high graduation dance. At any rate, we had an appointment with destiny six weeks away in early June of that year.

I cannot discredit the other two members

60

of the group. They actually possessed some talent. But I was the leader and gave the group no cohesion or sense of direction. We practiced at whim over the six weeks, finally securing a compendium of sixteen songs that we could play at the drop of a hat. We mostly mastered songs from the Jimi Hendrix library, like "Hey Joe" and "Purple Haze," which not only did not fit my prepubescent shrill, but also gave me an opportunity to butcher several legendary guitar solos. It also never occurred to me to add up the running time of all sixteen songs, or I would have realized that we had only forty-five minutes of actual music for a three-hour dance.

It also occurred to me the night before the dance that we had only small, rehearsal-size amplifiers. Add to that, we were a band of three, not four or five, and we were going to look silly being swallowed up by the expanse of the school stage. We also had no sound systems and no microphones. So less than twenty-four hours before the big gig, we began a scavenger hunt to borrow equipment.

Amazingly, we actually found some. There were a few well-established working bands in the area that loaned us equipment. We had several shoulder-height, professional-looking amplifiers, a couple of microphones, and the borderline look of a decent rock 'n' roll band.

What we didn't have was the sound of a decent rock 'n' roll band. Not only because of my muddy accompaniment on the guitar, not only because my voice was still yo-yoing back and forth between prepubescence and manhood, but mostly because I had forgotten to also grab the connecting cables for all the equipment we had borrowed from the other groups. So, all the impressive equipment — the amplifiers, the columns of speakers, the mixers, and the mikes — just sat on stage. It was an impressive sight, but none of it worked.

And, as you might have guessed, precisely forty-five minutes into the evening, we ran out of music. The Whiskey Rebellion exhausted its entire inventory of sixteen songs, and we had more than two hours left to play. As I strummed the last few chords to the final selection, I felt that twisted knot the captain of the ship gets when he realizes his vessel is sinking, and he has to ride it to the bottom. I wanted so badly to grab the microphone and scream that my dog had eaten our music.

Somehow we filled the rest of the evening by playing every song again and then again after that. I even made up lyrics to "Hey Joe" like "Hey Joe, what's your favorite color?" Anything to stretch it out. The seventh-graders barely danced. We watered down the reprise of our repertoire with extended drum solos, and we even started to improvise — or "jam," as I believe we called it. We just strummed and drummed until eleven o'clock mercifully arrived. There were no encores, they'd had enough. We received fifty dollars for the dance, and that was the total career earnings of the Whiskey Rebellion. We never played again, and I believe the world of rock 'n' roll is better for it.

The notion of thoughtful preparation evaded me in my youth and continued to elude me through college as well. I crammed for every exam, earning C-plus results for C-plus efforts. I accepted mediocrity.

What changed my laziness was the theater. I defined myself as an actor. That's what I wanted to be. An actor of any consequence *has to prepare.* Otherwise you don't know your lines, you don't know where to go on-stage, and you have nothing to bring to the character you have been given to portray. This is not to say that there are not lazy actors. There are plenty.

Perhaps because becoming an actor was so important to me — that was the reason I changed my habits. There is no feeling in the world like having to face an audience unprepared; it is worse than the fear of being naked in front of a crowd, which, oddly enough, is an actual psychological curiosity commonly called the Actor's Nightmare.

The Nightmare is both a dream and a lesson of comeuppance. It takes many shapes. The defining characteristic of the Actor's Nightmare is that you appear onstage ill-prepared or without your clothes.

My version has three distinct patterns. In the first, I'm an actor in a summer repertory company doing three plays. I'm quite accomplished in the first, I sort of know the lines for the second play, and I haven't a clue what the lines are for the third play. I fumble for words while the audience laughs me into a cold sweat and I wake up.

In the second version, I'm naked. Simple as that. I apparently develop a habit of forgetting to wear my clothes onstage. I'm also not quite aware of my little penchant until well into the evening's performance. Cold sweat redux.

Finally, there is the peculiar pattern I develop in my dreams where I leave the performance at the end of the first act and I forget to return. I leave for a perfectly valid reason, but one circumstance spills into another and eventually I remember that I forgot to return for the second act. This one is the worst.

The Actor's Nightmare is not restricted to thespians. Ask any professional and they will have their own version. Weathermen say they're naked in front of the wrong map. Doctors show up to the wrong surgery. Lawyers arrive for final summations unable to talk. This last one might not make the grade as a nightmare.

However they manifest themselves, these dreams are the distinctly human fear that our dog ate our homework — the fear of being ill-prepared. The paradox of this dream of inadequacy is that, in my experience, it occurs only in the minds of people who want to succeed. Underachievers sleep peacefully.

A few years back I had an opportunity to relive a portion of my life. I was given the rare chance of a do-over. Following my successful run on *Seinfeld* and thanks in part to the widespread publicity that surrounded the final episode, I was asked by my alma mater, Providence College, to give a concert along with the Rhode Island Philharmonic as part of the commencement activities for the graduating class.

There is nothing more terrifying to an artist than to sing with a symphony orchestra. Here's why: There is no room for error. If you are singing with a piano or even a few more pieces in a band and you slip up, the repair is pretty easy. They can vamp until you find each other again. But once a sixty-five-piece orchestra starts, it can't stop. Like a large boulder tumbling downhill, with you running in front of it. Each instrument is playing only a portion of each musical arrangement, which is all you hear onstage. It is their combined efforts that produce the fullness of the orchestral sound to the listener in the audience.

I had four months to prepare for this concert and no idea where to begin. I agreed to the performance because I had always wanted to sing with a symphony, and the chance to do it at the college where I began my theatrical aspirations made it as appealing as it was appropriate. Plus, I have a tendency (especially in my later years) to try things because I don't know that I can't do them.

I prepared for this ninety-minute concert with a focus and an energy that I had never before felt. I learned everything I could about the music I had chosen. I learned about music arrangers and arranging. I hired rehearsal musicians. I worked with my voice coach. Every available moment was spent thinking about this concert.

I will remember the entrance I made on the stage that night for the rest of my life. Unlike the early days of the ill-fated Whiskey Rebellion, I had done my homework this time, and I felt an empowerment that drove me through the evening. When the concert ended, more than three thousand people stood on their feet and applauded, and my eyes filled with tears. The tears were a mixture of emotions — partly the joy of sharing something so personally important with a college community that meant so much. But more important, the tears celebrated the fact that what I had imagined was what I had prepared for; and what I had prepared for was what I had accomplished. With these tears I quietly absolved myself of the earlier sins of the Whiskey Rebellion.

The world you will live in will have an unquenchable thirst for achievement, William. You will begin learning this in just a few years, as you watch some succeed and many fail around you. That's what Scoshi was saying in this note. To accept a goal means you must accept the responsibility of preparing for its accomplishment. In school it will be called homework. In life it will be called preparation. Any enduring success in your world will not be possible without it. If Christopher Columbum prepared his voyage in his world like I prepared his poster some five hundred years later, his ships would have sunk at the dock. If the Whiskey Rebellion in the 1790s was organized as haphazardly as its modern rock 'n' roll namesake, there would be no Kentucky bourbon. I'll leave you to draw your own conclusions on that.

If you prepare for life as thoroughly as you would for a symphony orchestra, life will reward you with the joy and the satisfaction of great music. If you choose to prepare less, you will accomplish less, and make no mistake about it, you will still hear a sound, but it will be a different one. It will be the distant sound of a dog, munching away on the absence of achievement.

ON SKUNKS, POISON IVY, AND LITTLE LEAGUE

Dear Little Pink Thing,

One night, years ago, I woke up in the middle of the night because I had to pee. I jumped down from the bed and went out the doggie-door into the darkness of the backyard. When I was finished I saw a little black-and-white thing in the corner of the yard. So I went over to sniff him out. Then he sprayed me with a funny smell. I went back into the house and jumped back on the bed. The smell woke Dad up and he got mad. He put me in the bathroom and made me sleep there for the night. I didn't know why — I didn't do anything wrong.

That was the night that I realized that life isn't fair. You have to make the best of it. Sometimes you just have to spend a night in the bathroom.

Let me clear this one up right away, lest I

look like the villain here. Scoshi didn't just "sniff" the skunk. He got in close enough to put his nose right up against the skunk's butt, judging from the perfectly formed circle of dripping yellow spray the size of a half-dollar he left on Scoshi's chest. What woke me up at 3 a.m. was my gag reflex kicking in. My eyes were watering and I could barely breathe. It was like using a chemical spill for an alarm clock.

The noxious scent of the spray was everywhere. On the bedding, on the bed, in the bedroom. All over the house and also all over my hands. I put Scoshi in the bathroom in an attempt to contain the collateral damage his smell was doing to my property value.

We define ourselves in moments of panic like this. I knew that tomato juice cuts the skunk stench, so at 3 a.m. I tore apart my bachelor-stocked kitchen with my toxic-smelling hands in search of a can of tomato juice.

What I found was a single-serving can of Clamato juice, an odd blend of tomatoes and clams, which at some point in my bachelorhood I apparently felt was a must-have. So in the early hours of that morning I had to make the strategic decision — was there enough tomato juice in the mix to cut the smell? I went with my instinct. I opened the can and poured it all over Scoshi in the tiled shower stall. As a result I had a dog that smelled like skunk, tomatoes, and clams.

In Hollywood, where I lived at the time, there is always some store open at all times of the day. So I threw on a pair of old, paint-crusted jeans and a torn T-shirt. It was a fashion ensemble that complemented my bed-head hairdo and one that I didn't mind discarding immediately after. I hopped in the car, added the smell of skunk to the steering wheel, and went off into the night in search of tomato juice at all costs.

I found an all-night convenience store just off Hollywood Boulevard, in one of its many less-than-prosperous neighborhoods, as evidenced by the large group of vagrants that had gathered to finish off a bottle or two on the steps. One of them tried to hit me up for some change on the way in only to turn his face away and wrinkle his nose as the odor of skunk wafted past him. Inside the store I found the last two bottles of tomato juice, which I brought up to check-out. The man at the register spoke badly broken English, but used what words he had available to tell me that I stank. Given the way I looked, the way I smelled was probably the perfect complement, so I didn't offer any explanation. I decided to let him live with the assumption that I was using my last five dollars to knock off a couple of bottles of tomato juice with my boys outside.

Scoshi did spend the rest of that night in the bathroom. The concentration of skunk odor didn't leave the house for a month, and I was reminded of that little black-and-white varmint every time I put my hands on my smelly steering wheel all the way up until the time six months later when I sold the car.

I wrote in my first book that I didn't understand what purpose was served by the existence of skunks. I still don't think this point can be overstated. I don't comprehend how their presence on this green earth helps to complete God's Great Plan or the fragile balance of nature.

I feel the same way about poison ivy.

The night that Scoshi described was not the last time that he got logo-ed by a backyard skunk. It has happened several times since. But judging from the note he left under the foot of the Big Blue Elephant, it was this first christening that affected him quite deeply. He was victimized by a skunk and then banished from the bed to the bathroom. It was the first time that it occurred to him that, even for a dog, life isn't all that fair.

I was introduced to the inequity of life in first grade, when our teacher, Miss Cox, would make the entire class stay after school because a handful of students were caught talking while she was out of the room. This became almost a daily practice. The same students talked and we all stayed after school. I was pretty much a model student back then, with a healthy respect for authority, so the repeated group punishment traumatized me for most of the year. But looking back on the experience now, it was an early lesson in the sometimes abysmal difference between justice and fairness. Justice was served because the letter of the law held that there was to be no talking when she was out of the room. The equitable punishment upheld the standard.

Fairness is what fell by the wayside, however. The blindness of justice failed to distinguish between the innocent and the guilty. Fairness, I have come to learn, is justice with compassion.

Sometimes the inequities of life operate outside a system of justice and fairness. Sometimes bad things just happen. Sometimes the deck just seems stacked against us. When I was in third grade, my heart was stolen by a very smart blonde named Henrietta. She was easily the smartest girl in the class — that's what I mean by smart blonde. (Prior to puberty kicking in, I always went for the smart girls.) I even was able to finagle a seat in front of her in class, and I always wore my best shirts, so that, even though it was only from the rear, I looked smart. I was very shy, but managed a cordial relationship all through the year. When the graded test papers were passed down the row, I always got to see hers first — and it was always an A or number near 100, and I was very proud of my girl. I always smiled at her as I passed it back, but we rarely spoke.

One afternoon in late spring my class was singing during our weekly music lesson. The song was "Old Folks at Home," a big, big Stephen Foster hit during the Civil War period. I was listening to Henrietta sing behind me in her pretty soprano. Brains and a voice, she had it all. But a sudden noise stopped the music. It was a guttural retching sound followed by a fluid blow. In an instant the class went silent as Henrietta lurched forward and threw up all over me.

I was wearing a very smart paisley print of

every fall color imaginable, so it was impossible to assess the damage. In fact, no one seemed to notice that she had vomited all over me. My back arched from the moment of impact and my arms flailed out in a near-crucifixionlike pose. The teacher evacuated the classroom to the auditorium to continue music class. Despite my protestations, I couldn't seem to get her attention. So I had to walk to the auditorium in a shirt soaked with Henrietta's lunch. Only when the teacher noticed that no one would walk near me did she come to inspect the problem. She summoned the principal, who led me to the showers, called my mother, and sent me home early.

Our relationship was never the same after that incident, during the last few weeks of class. She was embarrassed, and the innocence of my feelings for her would be forever mixed with the sound of her gag reflex. Our family moved across town that summer, and I never saw her again. Yes, life can change in an instant, and sometimes life is unexpectedly unfair.

I got stung again by this simple truth a few years later, when I tried out for the West Hartford Little League baseball team. The team was called Exchange, a name that baffles me to this day. Another team was called Retailers. I get the feeling that someone decided that if they couldn't find a local business to sponsor a team they would turn to the dictionary and name the teams after fiscal concepts.

Baseball was not just big in our household; it was apocalyptic. We were a Boston Red Sox family, more than just fans. It defined us by our tribal allegiance to a team that was named after a bold fashion accessory. I watched every game that was on television, and listened to every game that was on the radio. I knew all the players and their statistics. I was a student of the game. Now I was going to be a player of the game.

The tryouts for Exchange were held at a local school on a cloudy Saturday morning in early April. Parents dropped off their kids in the parking lot and we all made our way out to the back of the school to the baseball field with our baseball gloves in tow.

One parent, a father, remained. I remember this so distinctly. He was an older father, older than mine anyway. He had thick glasses and he held his son's hand as they walked out to the field. I remember thinking, even then, how nice it was for a father to accompany his son to these tryouts. He was the only one.

His son was a chip off the ol' block, and for all the wrong reasons. He had the same Coke-bottle glasses and was badly bucktoothed. He was skinny to the point of looking undernourished and underdeveloped. Worse than any of that, he had a baseball glove that looked brand-new without even a hint being worked in. Even his cap seemed to hang unhappily on his head.

I don't know his name. I never did. We were given numbers by the coaching staff that morning and that's the way they referred to us all day. After all, this wasn't a team practice, these were tryouts, and the numbers added to the antiseptic and impersonal feeling of the day.

We went through all sorts of drills — running, catching, throwing, and hitting — to test our baseball skills. We broke into two teams and played a scrimmage game. I had a double in my only at-bat. Well, almost a double. I was thrown out by a mile trying to stretch a single into an extra-base showcase. I performed well in my drills, I thought; I ran without falling, caught without dropping, and threw without missing.

I can't say the same for the little boy with the Coke-bottle glasses. He was a mess. He couldn't run, he dropped every fly ball with his spanking new glove, which he used like a deflector shield and threw *worse* than a girl. In the game he flailed at the ball with the bat, which was clearly too heavy for him to negotiate. He swung late and struck out each time he went to the plate. It broke my heart as I looked over at the stands to see his father, the Only Dad Who Stayed, witnessing such a slaughter of innocence. I remember him watching it all through his thick glasses in total calm, almost as though it didn't really matter.

No one paid much attention to this boy, except me. His noticeable lack of skills made him oddly invisible to those searching for athletes. Off in the prairies, when the bulls begin to run and the testosterone begins to swirl, the meek always fall by the wayside. It is much the same in Little League. The herd separates into haves and have-nots pretty quickly; it is not cool to associate with the uncoordinated, "unco's," as they were known in our young vernacular. Any association with them sent the wrong message to the coaches, who were silently eyeing all of us, looking for approved flesh. But my heart ached for this kid, so I said hi while we were waiting our turn to bat. That's all, just hi. There wasn't much else to add. I couldn't say, "How's it going?" Because even he knew it wasn't. He was a dead man barely walking, and we all knew it. And I'm sure the Only Dad Who Stayed knew it too.

By four o'clock in the afternoon, the tryouts and coaches' summit had ended. They were ready to announce who would be playing for Exchange that season. A couple of parents who had returned for pickup duty had begun to trickle in toward the stands to join the Only Dad Who Stayed. The coaches had us form a straight line, almost execution-style, along the first-base line. It seemed almost appropriate that way — that the boy with the Coke-bottle glasses would finally and mercifully be put out of his misery. But I still felt sad knowing what was about to happen. I remember sneaking a peek over at him, wondering what the inevitable felt like. It was as though, for one moment in time, I knew the future.

The head coach said that he would call the numbers of the players who made the Exchange team and for them to step forward. If your number wasn't called, you should stand alone for a moment to let the shock and consequences settle in, then walk off the field and begin to endure the rest of your miserable life. All right, he didn't say that, but he did add some innocuous disclaimer that we were all winners and something about how difficult the decision was to make. Buried in that nonsense was a dagger that he was about to bury into the heart of a little boy with Coke-bottle glasses, and all I could do was stand there on the first-base line and absorb some of the pain.

Slowly and deliberately the coach read the numbers from his list. Gradually another line formed in front, made of youngsters who had passed muster. As I waited for my call to join them I looked to the stands. The Only Dad was still there, his chin resting on his arms, which rested on his knees. He sat shrouded by the raincoat that he had worn since the early morning when this all began. His expression was still; he peered out through his thick glasses at his son, waiting for a number that would never be called. It wasn't.

Nor was mine.

In the chill of the late April afternoon, I stood alone for a moment to let the shock and consequences settle in. But they wouldn't. There had to have been a mistake. Maybe I was too busy looking at the Only Dad in the stands to pay attention to my own number. I pushed my way through the huddle of the fortunate to find the huddle of coaches with their clipboards. I asked the head coach to check his list again because I didn't hear my number and I did everything pretty well and I almost had a double and I knew everything about the Boston Red Sox and if I wasn't on the list then I'd have to walk off the field and begin to endure the rest of my miserable life.

It's not there, son, I'm sorry.

Somewhere in my preoccupation with how unfair life can be to young boys, that some are haves and some are have-nots, it failed to occur to me that on that cold gray day in April, the little boy with the Coke-bottle glasses and I could both be have-nots.

My baseball glove hung limply by my side; it felt strangely foreign to me and no longer a worthy weapon. As I left the field, I walked past the stands, now empty. The Only Dad Who Stayed had finally left with his son. In the front of the school in the parking circle, where the other parents were waiting, I saw the two of them as they were getting into their car. The Only Dad had been holding his son's spanking new glove, still barely soiled. Before he got into the car he tossed the glove back across the hood to his son with the Coke-bottle glasses. He caught it.

Oh sure, I thought, *now you can catch.* It made me feel worse.

My father was parked in the circle, waiting with the car running. As I opened the door, he could see it in my eyes. The question "How did it go?" was not necessary. I sat in silence looking straight ahead. I know my father said something to me, but I have no memory of his words. I was beyond consolation, still trying to absorb the sting of not being able to make Exchange, a team that wasn't even good enough to have a sponsor and had to be named after the nonathletic concept that all goods were ultimately returnable. My eyes were so full of tears that they finally exploded, and I cried all the way home. I missed dinner that night, preferring to beat my pillow and cry on my bed. I was no longer concerned about the little boy with the Coke-bottle glasses.

I don't think I'm wrong to say that this incident brought a very promising baseball career to a skidding halt. I never tried out for Little League again. From then on and even to this day, my glove has been retired to some dusty spot in the garage, and I rely on the Boston Red Sox to deliver that singular joy from the game of baseball.

It did introduce me, yet again, to the notion that life isn't fair. I am reminded of this every time I see pictures of the hollow eyes of children in Africa near starvation.

Why them? I am also (albeit less profoundly) reminded of it when I continually catch my toe on the end of the bed as I make my way to the bathroom in the middle of the night. *Why me?*

Life is not just unfair in cases of deficiency, but sometimes in abundance as well. There are people who have won the lottery more than once. I have seen gamblers bring a casino to its knees without breaking. I have occasionally driven the length of Santa Monica Boulevard without having to stop at a red light. I have found a crinkled-up twenty-dollar bill in a pair of old jeans I no longer wear. But I never say, *Why me?* in these instances. We tend to think of the inequity in life from the perspective of the have-nots rather than the haves. Sometimes we do get more than we deserve.

I often wonder what life would be like if it were fair. What if we got exactly what we deserved? There would be no skunks or poison ivy. I would never have stayed after school. I would have been cocaptain of my Little League team, along with a kid who had thick glasses and protruding front teeth. I would have gotten every role I auditioned for. I would not have lost so many friends through accidents and disease.

But if life were fair, it would be a life

without growth and perspective. There is meaning in suffering, as difficult as it is to endure. From it we learn humility and persistence. There is appreciation in abundance. From it we realize that life is full of grace as well.

Much as we depend on gravity to provide weight, we need suffering and abundance to give life a sense of context. Without gravity there would be no resistance, and everything would have the same weightlessness, floating aimlessly without distinction. A mountain grows tall and gives us a better and better view the more it moves against the resistance of the earth.

It is a pretty philosophy to regard suffering as an opportunity for growth, but it does not fill the stomach of a starving child, and I have no answer for that. I believe that God can do all things, but I have come to realize through personal experience that sometimes He does not. I believe there is a plan that is beyond my comprehension that allows a place for catastrophic human suffering for reasons that reason will never understand.

If we accept that unfairness is inevitable as long as we are alive, we can shift our focus to the far more important issue — how do we cope with suffering, both our own and in our compassion for the suffering of others?

William, I hope you take to heart this piece of advice, as it has helped me cope with every instance of personal hardship: *You are not your circumstances.* I'll say it again: *You are not your circumstances.* What happens to you, good and bad, is not the essence of who you are. Your circumstances are external to you; don't invite them in. They are unwelcome guests; they will try to make a victim of you. You will paralyze yourself with fear and depression if you let the unfairness of life become part of who you are. Conversely, you will become vain and arrogant if you become absorbed by the abundance and good fortune that life will also bring your way. I've often looked to Scoshi, a pillar of self-possession in moments of both feast and famine, when attempting to gain perspective in life: Scoshi is grateful when a chewie comes his way and doesn't dwell on it when I forget to give him one. He is the same sweet dog sleeping on my pillow as he is sleeping with the scent of skunk on a bathroom floor. He never becomes his circumstances.

It is not what happens to us in life, my boy; it is what we do about it. And that is the second element of coping with a world that is inherently unfair. How you react to both adversity and prosperity will determine your character, and, in many cases, your circumstances.

Sometimes you will realize, as I have, that the unfairness of rejection is simply protection in disguise. I have lived with much rejection. I have been cut from teams because I was not good enough to compete. I have lost many roles as an actor that I was not ready to command. I have had my heart broken by people who were not good for my life. I allow myself to mourn those losses for a day, and no more. Then I must move on.

There will be times when I will seem unfair to you as your father. There will be times when I will have to mix the firm hand of discipline with the gentle arms of my embrace. Life will seem unfair to you. But I will try to give you visible standards of behavior to live by, and I will try to live by those standards myself.

I hope you dedicate yourself, Will, to leaving the world a fairer place by taking responsibility for your actions. Judge others by what they do, not by who they are. Do not shun others or compare yourself to them, and be careful about associating with groups. More often than not, groups are less mature than the individuals in them because the heart of their purpose is to ostracize others. It happens as often in life and politics as in the schoolyard, and it is equally as cruel. For there to be an *us,* there has to be a *them.*

It is perfectly okay, however, to hate the New York Yankees.

So think less about the life you deserve, and enjoy the one you have. The same unfairness in life that left Scoshi to sleep that night on the bathroom floor is the same unpredictable life that is full of skunks, poison ivy, and the occasional misjudgments of Little League coaches. It is the same inequitable life that is sometimes of prejudice, cruelty, and human tragedy. But it is also the same wonderful life that, by the grace of God, brought you to me.

And I welcome it all, William, for that one sacred instance of grace.

A Good Gorilla
Is Tough to Find

Dear Little Pink Thing,

I lived most of my life without a special toy. So did Dad. Then one day I found my Gorilla. I just knew it was special. Just about the same time Dad found Mom. I think he was just trying to copy me. But it worked out pretty well. In fact, I like her more than him.

Every night I sleep on my Gorilla. Dad sleeps next to Mom. We all sleep together. I hope you find someone special, too. But take your time and choose wisely. A good Gorilla is tough to find. Never choose one irresponsibly, and know what you are doing if you give one up.

Yes, Scoshi finally did find someone special. The Gorilla is small and stuffed, yellow with orange stripes — a bit different from most Gorillas, but I suspect, perhaps, that is part of the attraction. For all the years I've had him, Scoshi was never before attracted to any particular toy. You could toss almost anything at him and get the same lukewarm response.

For example, one Sunday afternoon while I was living in Malibu many years ago, I took Scoshi to the beach for a little man and dog, surf and sand commingling. I had just bought a red doggie Frisbee, one with a hole in the center for easier grasping. I led Scoshi down to a popular beachfront to let him chase the waves for a bit before we got down to some serious toss and fetch.

Coincidentally, a bit farther up on the fairly crowded beach, Pierce Brosnan had set up camp on the sand with his family and his two beautiful golden retrievers. He was throwing tennis balls into the surf and the dogs were swimming out eagerly to retrieve them. Pierce had already raised the bar in Hollywood pretty much beyond my reach, and now his dogs were doing it to Scoshi. But I decided to let him have his day in the court of public opinion.

I hurled the red Frisbee with an admirable snap of the wrist down the surf line and it sailed about ten feet off the ground, gliding for several hundred feet, when it came to a rest. At the same moment I yelled loud enough for everyone to hear, including the two golden Brosnanian retrievers, *"GO GET IT, SCOSH!"* He sat next to me panting and looking down the beach, very much admiring the spirit of my effort. He also seemed to enjoy the hundred-yard walk we took to pick it up, totally unaware of all chuckles coming from the many blankets up on the sand, especially from the Brosnanian retrievers. Perhaps it is no coincidence that Pierce's career and mine have never crossed paths after that humiliating afternoon at the beach.

So it was with Scoshi's inability to commit to any special object until the appearance last year of the yellow and orange-striped Gorilla. I'm not even sure how it arrived at the house, under the multicolored pile of soft, stuffed toys in his white wicker basket. But one night there was a yellow Gorilla on my wife's pillow — a sort of wedding night, apparently. It has never left that spot for several years.

Today the Gorilla is worn a bit from years of nocturnal cuddling. Scoshi sleeps with his head resting on the Gorilla's stomach, which has now become comfortably thin of stuffing and forms a nice little pocket for his chin. It is the easy fit of a couple blessed with permanence, and they celebrate their history every night when the lights go out.

Will, I hope you find someone special, too. I hope you find someone as special as your mother, someone with an ease of humor, gentle on the eyes, and with the heart of a saint. But I hope you find many special relationships in life because, when all is said and done, it is our relationships that matter most. A real man needs real friends.

I hope, too, that you find other parents. I know that remark may startle you, but I mean it from the heart. We will never leave you, but your mother and I can teach you only so much. We are limited in what we know and by our fears, and you will need to grow beyond what we can expose to you. Eventually what we say will become numb to you, and you will need to hear the truths of life in different ways. It is not a bad thing at all; it is the normal route of developing your sense of self. Because of that you must *re-parent* again and again, and you must embrace these new parents each time they appear.

Your new parents will come to you in many forms and appear as unexpectedly as the yellow Gorilla. They may be teachers, coaches, authors, celebrities (God forbid), or other people whom you come to admire for their special gifts or a meaningful message. As Scoshi says, choose them wisely and take their advice to heart, for they are on this earth to help you as surely as your mother and I are.

My first memory of another parent was the late actor Lloyd Bridges, who starred in *Sea Hunt,* the underwater action series in the late fifties and sixties. Lloyd was my first exposure to hero worship. At the age of four, I became obsessed with scuba diving and its potential to rid the world of evil, at least the world beneath the sea. I had my father make a mock-scuba outfit. My little red fire hydrant–shaped piggy bank became my breathing tank, strapped to my back with a belt. I had a little blue Speedo bathing suit and goggles, and my flippers were my father's black high-top basketball sneakers. Every Sunday night after *Sea Hunt* aired, I'd go in for my bath and re-create the entire episode.

I still thank Lloyd for introducing me to acting. And to the notion that I must use my powers for good and not evil.

Years later, when I was about fourteen or so, my father took a course from Dale Carnegie, the famous corporate trainer who taught the dynamics of public speaking and influence in business. I read every book my father brought home; Carnegie quickly emerged as my second "new parent." His books probably taught me as much about being an actor as any coach I have ever had. But they taught me more about the power of self-confidence in developing good speaking skills, as well as to look for the positive qualities in everyone and compliment them. I still read my Carnegie library to this day.

A few years after that, when I became more drawn to public speaking, I began listening to the legendary broadcaster Paul Harvey religiously. I was drawn to the commentator's unusual style and his mastery of the dramatic pause. He had such a colorful mastery of language, and it was my introduction to the importance of using the correct words to shape my ideas. I actually won several public-speaking awards during my high school years by keeping his unique style of communication in my head.

My most important re-parenting experience, however, came later in life. At the age of thirty-six, I met an elderly man and his wife on a cruise across the Atlantic. I was onboard working, filming scenes for a television pilot. The man and his wife were taking one of their many vacations around the world. His name was Barry Garfield, and he and his wife, Elaine, were delightful company. We would dine together each evening. Barry was a loving man with children of his own, and possessed the wonderful gift of mentoring to others. He genuinely cared about young people. He had sponsored many through college, and provided financing for others so that they could purchase their first homes. (He had amassed a fortune by executing a wonderfully simple idea: He had created *the* cross-reference guide for tires and automobiles. It was the bible of the automotive industry, and he had the monopoly on it.) For all his success, mostly, Barry was about joy. He communicated joy in his smile, in his example, and his relationships with everyone around him.

Something that Barry said to me one night changed my life forever. We were on the leg of the cruise that brought us north of the Arctic Circle, past Iceland, on the third week in June, a time of the year in these latitudes when the sun never sets. It was a particularly appropriate surrounding for what he was about to tell me. It was after dinner and we were sitting on the top deck of the ship enjoying a glass of wine as we watched the sky enjoy the permanent light. Barry leaned into me, put his hand on my arm, and, in a gruff and gentle voice, said this to me:

John, you have two choices in life: You can have an ordinary life, or you can have an extraordinary life. That's it.

As simple as it may seem, this was one of the most profound ideas I had ever entertained. He went on to explain that an extraordinary life has nothing to do with money or power, but it has everything to do with the power of your choices. In an environment of opportunity, we are responsible for both the direction and the quality of the results of our lives.

That was the night I committed to the idea of an extraordinary life. It was a personal transformation that I will always remember because of both the midnight sun and the kindness of an elderly man whose only purpose was to add meaning to the lives of others. Barry and I remained close until his death several years later. I mourned his loss deeply, as I would have my own grandfather. In many ways, that's who he was, a *grand father.*

Will, I wish you many parents in your life, mentors who will join me in giving you examples of excellence. It is so much easier to be a champion when you are surrounded by them. Sadly, it is so much more difficult for people to succeed when they are encircled by the ordinary.

In my wedding vows to your mother, Will, I promised her an extraordinary life. I make that same commitment to you as my son.

Somewhere from the mist, a Gorilla will magically appear on your pillow as well, my boy. There will be someone special in your life, perhaps more than one. My only advice is to be sure that the ones you choose share the values that you will have worked so hard to establish for yourself. Similar standards breed mutual respect, and beyond love, every good bond is built on respect. It is easier to partner for life when you have found your best friend.

Please take to heart the warning that Scoshi wrote in his note to you. *Never choose a Gorilla irresponsibly, and know what you are doing when you give one up.* The human heart is the most fragile thing. It is easy to open up and easier to wound. When I recall the great regrets of my life, they are not about the money I've lost, places I never went, or people I never met. They are not about things I never had or jobs that I never got. They are about the hearts that I've hurt and the sadness that I have left behind in my track. You can forgive yourself, as others will forgive you, but the memory of the wounds you cause will always remain. A heart is a precious gift. Treat it with that regard.

Right now you are interested in women only inasmuch as they can feed you and change your diapers. I suppose as I grow older I will develop that interest as well. But I hope you look to your mother as an example of the gift of femininity. And I hope you look upon the love and the laughter she and I share as a proper model for you as well.

I have lived alone, my son, and I have lived with another. I can honestly attest that I am a better man for having your mother in my life. For me, two is better than one. She completes me, as your presence in our lives completes us both. It has taken me a long time to find that wholeness. Scoshi is right, so take heed. *A good Gorilla is tough to find.*

WHEN ALL IS SAID AND DONE, MORE WAS SAID THAN DONE

Dear Little Pink Thing,
   Don't bark unless you mean it. And don't stop until they know you mean it.

I sat with this one for a while, Will. Not because the meaning was that obscure — it wasn't. It was, in fact, so simple — Scoshi wants you to have the courage of your convictions.

For several nights, though, I lay awake thinking about this note. The quiet of the night, deprived of light and distraction, often brings contemplation instead of sleep. The more I thought about the message the more my mind flooded with memories of early obstacles, confrontations, victories, and disappointments in my life. I was consumed by a sense of wholeness and peace at what I had achieved, yet was overwhelmingly sad at what I had failed to do. The note brought with it a silent epiphany for me because it begged for such a brutal answer to such a fundamental question: *Are you a man of your word?*

Indeed, I was not. At least for a significant portion of my life. I was not genuinely a man of my word until one specific incident, which changed the direction and the purpose of my life. That change has made all the difference. I'd like you to know that story, Will. It's a tale of two boys.

The first boy was named Bob. Of the many talents Bob was blessed with, the most compelling was that he had one of the most engaging personalities combined with a genuine humility that let him pass off all his outstanding accomplishments with a smile and a simple shrug of his athletic shoulders. Everybody loved Bob.

He was an exceptional student at Kingswood-Oxford School in West Hartford, always achieving high honors without seeming to make much of it. He was more interested in doing an impression of the French teacher than he was in actually learning the language, yet he won many academic awards.

Bob captained three sports during his high school years. He was an exceptional soccer player, as well as an extraordinary talent at tennis, which he played at the varsity level as only a freshman. But he put that aside one year to start all over in a new sport, lacrosse, which seemed to appease his take-no-prisoners approach to the athletic field. He later captained that sport as well.

He went to Amherst College, one of the most difficult schools to gain admission to. During his four years there he was an outstanding scholar-athlete, earning honors and becoming a two-sport captain, despite being sidelined by many injuries from his aggressive play. Everyone at Amherst knew him and loved him.

What made him achieve so much, so consistently, was that Bob *did what he said he was going to do.* It was as simple as that. Bob lived life on his terms.

What makes his part of the story more interesting is that he had one dream in life. If you had asked Bob at the age of nine or at nineteen what he wanted to do, he would've given the same answer. He wanted to be a doctor. More specifically, he wanted to be a family practitioner, a medical field that has become increasingly vacated in favor of more lucrative specialties. He wanted to treat families because he related to people so well.

You might think Bob's life was one effortless transition to the next. Not so. Bob was not admitted to medical school.

Despite a fairy-tale résumé as a scholar-athlete, despite a college record of leadership with the highest recommendations of his teachers and friends, Bob did not gain admittance to a single medical school. He had applied at the time when all institutions of higher learning were under intense pressure to fill minority quotas. For the first time in his life, Bob was left behind.

A man's character is defined not by what happens to him in life, but what he does about it. Bob would not be denied his dream.

For two years Bob returned to his high school alma mater, where he taught science and coached several sports. He was as extraordinary as a teacher and coach as he had been as a student and athlete. He had such an accessible way about him that endeared him to the entire student body.

Each year he applied again to medical school. Each year he was denied. After several years of persistence, finally he was accepted by a school in Ohio.

Bob's life was one that deserved a happy ending. He spread happiness wherever he went. The world around him was always happier, friendlier, and gentler for his presence. The world of medicine desperately needed a man who was as comfortable with healing as he was with a joke.

On a late August night at the end of his first year of the medical education he so desperately pursued, Bob was killed instantly in a horrific head-on crash with a drunk driver. How sadly ironic that he died on a hometown road that he frequented often as a youth.

Bob was my best friend growing up, which makes me the other boy in this tale. I will remember the call that I took from his mother that following morning. Her words were barely intelligible through her grief. Even to this day, nearly thirty years later, my fingers still gnarl as I search for the words to describe my sadness.

It was a tragedy of potential that went unfulfilled. So many before me had lost friends, but the world had lost someone capable of greatness. *What made Bob particularly great was that he always did what he set out to do. He had the courage of his convictions.*

I don't hold up my end of the tale as nobly as Bob did. I was never his equal as a student and certainly not his peer in sports. We shared the same sense of humor and that is how we bonded. We made each other laugh.

We also shared the intensity of our dreams. His was for medicine, mine for theater. Bob wanted to be a doctor as fiercely as I was wanted to be an actor. We defined ourselves by our dreams.

Where we differed was in our persistence. Bob persevered, and I buckled like tinder under the weight of my fears.

I had immersed myself completely in the theater in high school and college. But when the time came to gather myself, pack my bags, and head to the Big Apple to ply my craft on the chilly blocks of Broadway, I folded like a frightened schoolgirl. I had no idea how to succeed in the business I had dreamed about and by which I had defined myself since the age of three. So while Bob was teaching because he had been denied admission, I went into public relations for six years. Make no mistake, public relations is an exciting and noble profession. But Bob chose teaching biology to stay close to his goal while he persisted in his purpose; I entered public relations because I was afraid to fail as an actor. Every morning that I went to work, I knew I was heading down the wrong path. These were some of the most difficult years of my life, and every day I tried to make sense of my misdirection.

Bob's death was a catalyst for me, the most powerful I have ever faced. I could not allow myself the experience of this person and miss the meaning. Bob had always been a champion, but I could not say the same for myself.

It was while I was driving to his funeral that I made a promise to myself. I was going to spend two years preparing myself for the business of acting, and I was going to New York. (At the time I was director of public relations for the American National Red Cross in Connecticut.) I gave myself a date — the first week in September 1981. It was Bob's death that gave me my life back. I had lost my bark, in Scoshi's terms — but I was going to get it back.

I took a train from Hartford to New York that following week and found an acting coach. I would take that train at 6 a.m. every Saturday for the following two years without fail, in snow or rain, to spend the full day training in the theater district in Manhattan. I downsized my car, my apartment, and my life to begin an aggressive savings plan. I found a singing coach to work on my voice. On Friday nights I would leave my public relations job and drive forty miles across the border into Massachusetts in a cheap, rebuilt VW Beetle to be a singing waiter at a Rodeway Inn Motel restaurant along the Interstate. I did it not for the meager pay (somehow I seemed to earn less than a regular waiter), but for the experience of singing and performing. I performed with a local theater group and anywhere else I got a chance. I also began running, something I hated. I did it for the exercise, but more for the mental conditioning. When my lungs would start to burn and my legs got heavy, I would scream to myself, *How bad do you want it?* It was a two-year theatrical boot camp. The memory of Bob and the way he lived his life was all I had to drive me.

My parents drove me to New York City that Sunday evening in September 1981. Two weeks earlier I had resigned from my job. We had just dropped my sister off earlier that day farther up the Hudson where she was beginning college. They felt infinitely more at ease about that part of the trip. The car was eerily quiet as we made our way through the drizzle down the West Side Highway in the city. My father pulled up to the single-room-occupancy hotel on the Upper West Side. Together we took the three suitcases and two boxes — all that remained in my downsized life — and brought them to my room on the fourth floor.

My mother remained in the car. She was not happy with my decision to do this, and would have been a lot less happy if she saw the conditions in which I would now be living. A quarter of the bed was missing — as though someone had bitten a large piece off in the final stage of starvation. The sheets and bedding were tucked in around it. There were dead insects of the roach variety on the windowsills. The bathroom was shared, and the shower curtain toxic.

My father put the last of my suitcases on what remained of the bed. He slowly shook his head and without much ceremony said, "I hope you know what you're doing." I went to the window to watch him get in the car. I can only imagine what he said to my mother. Perhaps he said nothing at all, sparing her the details. I watched as the taillight disappeared down West 79th Street. The rain was coming down steadily now, adding to the dreariness of the welcome. I turned and looked at the three suitcases stacked by two boxes on three quarters of a bed. I walked over to them, sat down, and cried.

My end of the tale is much happier than Bob's. I began my career as an actor only forty-eight hours later, in a poorly executed and blissfully unmemorable musical. It was the beginning of a nearly thirty-year career.

But to begin it, I had to borrow from Bob's commitment to life, a sense of purpose that I could never have mustered on my own. If I have succeeded in this world at all, it is because I once stood on his athletic shoulders.

Becoming a man of your word becomes easier with practice, as it was for me in the years that followed the move to New York. Your bark gets stronger with practice and commitment. The larger lesson, though, is this: I can no longer verbalize something unless I intend to do it. That is a promise I have made to myself, and it has been the single source of success for me. The discipline of carrying the ball across the goal line becomes a habit that gets easier the more you exercise it.

What is tragic for me now is the idea of empty promises. We hear them all the time. They are the things we intend to do, for ourselves and others; the ideas, the dreams, the ambitions spoken so freely. But things that ultimately go undone.

In each of us I firmly believe there is a call to greatness — greatness within the perspective of our abilities. What is great for me may not be right for you. And yet, I also believe that the best ideas still lie dormant in the minds of people who, sadly, think everyone has a better idea than they do. As Scoshi would say, *They live life without a bark.*

I have written it before, and it bears mentioning again: What we daydream about is actually our call to greatness. Our persistent fantasies are not idle pipe dreams. They are one of the few ways God can communicate with us. The first time you commit to the completion of a dream is the beginning of a lifelong journey of achievement. Ask anyone who has crossed the finish line of a marathon what empowerment feels like.

Sadly, Will, you will never know Bob. He would have been the rough-and-tumble "uncle" who would have tossed you about. He would have sat with me on the sidelines of every game you ever played. He might have even been your doctor. And you would have learned from him the same truth that I did by example. You can be a successful man only if you are a man of your word.

Sadly, too, you will probably not know Scoshi. But in his note to you was the same message. Your word is your bark. Protect it, for it is precious. And when you give it, make the world aware.

The Authentic Walk

Dear Little Pink Thing,

Last year Dad did something really dumb. We lived in a New York apartment while Dad was acting on Broadway. He bought a square patch of grass in a box, placed it on the floor in the living room, and he expected me to pee on it instead of taking me downstairs for a walk. I never used it, except once I took a nap on it. Dad doesn't realize that just because the grass is real, that doesn't make the walk authentic.

I always wondered why he never used that box of grass. Now I know. I might have felt the same way if someone had, say, replaced my glass of pinot noir on the table next to me with grape juice. I also realize now how silly I must have looked trying to winter-garden a patch of grass in a New York City apartment.

His conclusion, though, is actually profound. The grass was real, but it was an inauthentic substitute for a walk. A walk is not so much about the chance for Scoshi to relieve himself as it is a moment of bonding between him and me. It is a chance to reestablish his turf and erase the scent of ogres that have tried to pee on his sacred spots. It is about celebrating the gift of smell, as peculiar as some smells may be. Yes, Scoshi was reminding me that there can sometimes be a striking difference between reality and authenticity.

The way I have come to see it, authenticity is reality with meaning. Grape juice is *real,* but my glass of pinot noir is *authentic* because it is a product of a deeper human purpose. Understanding this distinction between the authentic and the inauthentic, I believe, is the difference between living an ordinary life and an extraordinary life.

My ridiculous and embarrassing attempt at sod farming in Manhattan notwithstanding, I take issue with Scoshi on the implication that I am insensitive to the desperate need for authenticity in life. I am so deeply sensitive to it, in fact, that it is a constant topic of many of the talks that I give around the country. But I am as surprised as I am grateful that Scoshi, too, felt that for William, this was a fundamental lesson of manhood.

I stumbled upon the notion of authenticity quite unexpectedly with, appropriately enough, a glass of pinot noir at 34,000 feet. I was traveling on another of my mind-numbing commutes between Los Angeles and New York about five years ago. Normally on long flights like these, I bury myself in stacks of reading material, pausing for an occasional nap or to look out the window and down at the stippling of small towns and endless quilt of circle-farms that seem to fill the endless void across the Midwest. I get a lot of thinking done at these times. Blame it on the altitude, blame it on the stillness, or blame it on the wine.

This particular trip I was sitting next to a man I have long admired, Bob Costas. Bob has had a distinguished career as both a sports commentator and a broadcast journalist. He is unique, I believe, in his ability to command attention on any topic. I also admire him because of his ease of delivery, his vocabulary, and the depth of his point of view. What can I say, I'm a fan.

I'm not sure if he knew who I was, nor did it seem important, as he was pretty easy to engage in conversation. He was as gracious and considerate as I had imagined him to be. We covered myriad topics, sports and beyond. After all, I had only five hours with him, so I had to squeeze out of him as many thoughts as possible.

I asked him a question I have asked many contemplative people: *What is the greatest challenge facing contemporary man?* His response came a moment after he carefully digested my query. *We are losing our sense of authenticity.*

I had never heard that term before, nor did I realize that we were at the stage of crisis. He went on to explain that we are losing our originality of thought and experience, not only culturally, but socially and intellectually, and it was quickly permeating every facet of contemporary life.

Our paths have not crossed since that afternoon on the plane. Perhaps they will again. If they do, I will remind him of how poignant his answer was.

Since then, I have taken many flights. I have sat in similar seats in similar planes and looked out the same windows over the same country below. I reflect often on what he said about the crisis of authenticity.

I believe that, as a culture, we have not suddenly lost authenticity as much as we have let it slip gradually away by making weaker and weaker choices. And because of this surrender, we are slowly giving away the possibility of experiencing authentic moments and living authentic lives.

An authentic moment is one that is greater than the sum of its parts, one that is deeper than the simplicity of its circumstances. Using the patch of grass would have addressed Scoshi's necessary function, but the walk embodied the function and the richness of experience. That's what makes the walk authentic. As you read these words and think about this definition, you may recall similar moments in your own life. Authentic moments are infused with meaning; they are often moments that define us. They are not typically grand moments, but ones that are specific and intensely personal. They are often the ones that are the most incommunicable.

I remember a late afternoon in our small college chapel during my senior year at school, as I struggled with what to make of my life. I remember the golden rays of the late-winter sunset piercing through the stained glass and the chapel was mottled with colored shadows. I was alone there. As I shifted my weight on the kneeler, the wooden pew would crackle and echo. The chapel had a deeper kind of silence, heavier than normal. It was the first time in my life that I truly felt the presence of God. It was not a typical church visit. It was made authentic because, perhaps for the first time, I was quiet enough to actually experience a moment of prayer.

I also recall fishing in the dusk-light of the midnight sun on a lake in western Alaska at two-thirty in the morning, back in 1994. I was several hundred miles from the nearest human being. I was humbled by the size of the landscape around me. The kelly green mountains and the clear-blue waters of the glacier lake seemed so much more important than I was at that moment. I was only borrowing a moment from them. They were there long before me and will remain there long after I am gone — and therein lay the authenticity of the moment. When we are surrounded by nature, we are in the presence of greatness that dwarfs our sense of self-importance. I promised myself I would always remember that moment, and I have.

I remember other moments that were not as quiet, but were equally as authentic. I recall the first time I sang professionally on-stage. The summer following my college graduation, I was hired to sing for the Rhode Island College Cabaret Theater, a popular summer venue in Providence. It was actually my first professional job in entertainment, albeit for a hundred dollars a week. That first night I stood offstage with a microphone in one hand and my nervous stomach with the other. I was going to sing a favorite of mine, a Sinatra ballad called "You Will Be My Music." The lights came up on stage, the audience hushed, the conductor dropped his arm, and the introduction began. Caught up in the spirit of the moment, I made my entrance by rushing up the four steps that led out to the mirrored circular stage, looking very much like Mr. Suave. Unfortunately, in my eagerness to entertain and be loved, the toe of my shoe caught the top of the last step to the stage and I started a slow-motion moment of stumbling that propelled me out to center stage, where I finally surrendered to gravity and fell flat on my face. Sinatra himself probably never got as many laughs as I did with that heartfelt ballad, but then I'm sure it never occurred to Old Blue Eyes to start singing facedown on the stage.

Another time, back in 2000, I was playing as a celebrity golfer in the Phoenix Open, easily one of the most popular tournaments on the PGA tour with a daily attendance of more than 100,000 people. On the third hole of the esteemed Tournament Players Club, I casually bent over to pick my ball out of the hole — and I split my pants from stem to stern. To make the situation more embarrassing, I was wearing black pants and white underwear. The contrast of colors made the gap impossible for anyone to miss. For the next fifteen holes, and next four hours I was a running joke and a source of hysteria for thousands in the gallery every time I bent over to tee up my ball or take it out of the hole.

In both instances I was the victim of happenstance. After all, I have discovered, there is nothing funnier than an actor who falls flat on his face or a celebrity golfer who rips his pants in front of thousands. To laugh at yourself, and to let others laugh with you, makes you realize that to be authentic you must enjoy that you are perfectly imperfect.

These are just a few of the authentic moments I have experienced. There are many more like them. They belong to me. They define me both with humor and with spirit. For better or worse, moments like these have added richness to the fabric of my life. They are my history.

Authentic moments strung together like so many oddly shaped pearls become an authentic life. This crisis of authenticity comes from our surrender to the inauthentic, to moments and experiences that are as pedestrian as the next. As I look out of the plane today, years after I first encountered the concept of authenticity, I see a different sight below me. I witness a sad and gradual homogenization of America. Great cities that once had specific identities are almost indistinguishable, made identical by layers of malls, restaurant chains, and civic centers. Small towns, too, with Main Streets, barbers, and toy stores, surrender to the sterile inevitability of Wal-Mart.

We are losing our precious sense of place. We are moving in to prepackaged communities, where every home looks the same. If you can't figure out how to decorate your living room, you can go next door and see how they did it. The humor in that observation makes me sad.

The irony of this shift is that it is not, at its heart, ill-intended. I think people want ease of living and ease of thinking. It is indeed the ease of economics to move all the stores from Main Street inside the controlled environment of a mall, or to ease them out altogether with a more economical super–department store. It is the ease of economics that builds all the homes at once from the same template and calls it, ironically, a development. It makes more homes available to many. It is even the ease of economics to eat prefabricated food at restaurant chains.

But ease comes at a cost, in my personal view, both individually and collectively as a culture. We can shop at the same stores and eat at the same restaurants. We can wear the same logos on our shirts and jeans. Ironically, the person whose name is logo-ed there doesn't know who we are or perhaps even care, and yet we wear the name as proudly as a badge. In fact, as I write this and look out over the top of my laptop to my feet, I can even see someone's name stitched on my socks.

As we submit to the synthetic, to the artificial, and to the prepackaged experience, I fear we are surrendering the chance to live authentically. And this is where I must, as a father, raise the flag of worry. I am reminded of an area near the house in which I lived in West Hartford, when I was ten. It consisted of a series of empty lots that were never developed and left to overgrow. These several acres of bushes and trees were known by all as the Bumps, probably as a testament to a poorly graded dirt road that cut the area in half. Every child in the neighborhood lived at the Bumps. Home was only where you went to eat and sleep. Almost every important moment of my life happened there that year. It was more than where I played. It was where I met my best friends, where I learned how to hide, where I got hurt, where I built a fort, where I learned to fight, and where I learned to negotiate. The Bumps was a discarded place, but an authentic place because on any given day it could become anything or anyplace, whatever our imaginations demanded. How ironic that a site so neglected and so common supported so much life.

The Bumps are gone today. I visited the area on a recent trip back to my hometown. A half dozen homes now stand on that hallowed ground. A perfectly paved road now cuts the area in half. There is no evidence of the field that was once there, and no evidence of the ghosts of youth that held it so precious.

In today's erosion of the authentic, places like the Bumps have become forgotten fields. Sadly, from what I have witnessed, they no longer seem necessary. They have been replaced, not by homes, but, in my opinion, Will, by video games — which buffer youngsters from any need for human contact, from any use of imagination, and render an authentic moment all but impossible. The dungeons we created in the

Bumps and the dragons we imagined were far more authentic than those on a video screen. I am reminded of the Bumps when I remember that while the authentic can be destroyed, it cannot be created.

What we seem to have lost as well are the authentic treasures that come from having hobbies. Video games and iPods have replaced them as well. Hobbies connect young people to the authentic; they are a way for them to embrace it with the odd collections of stamps and coins and model airplanes. Along with baseball cards, rocks, and tropical fish they are nothing but odd trinkets in themselves, but when they are carefully assembled or gathered together in the hands of a child they come alive as if by magic. And they are magic in their ability to educate, entertain, and inspire a young mind.

I've had every hobby possible. I mean that — all of them. I have collected everything imaginable — rocks, shells, stamps, coins, insects, butterflies, religious goods, comics, turtles, fish, and even Indian artifacts. I'm sure I've forgotten some.

As a nine-year-old with fresh money from my weekly allowance I would walk several blocks to the center of West Hartford every

Saturday morning, at a time and in a place when a nine-year-old could still do that. I was on my way to a small, second-floor storefront called the X-tra Nice Stamp and Coin Co. It was a dark, one-room hovel lit with a mixture of fluorescents on the ceiling and greenish red neon from the X-tra Nice sign in the window. A double-wide oak casement filled the center of the room with stacks of dark oak files lining the walls.

It was a mom-and-pop outfit. The pop was a bit gruff, a no-nonsense gentleman with thick glasses. The business of stamps and coins was his life. This truth was clear to tell from his academic demeanor. But he took kindly to me the more I came to his shop. I would spend hours there, asking to see the ancient treasures in his files. He grew wonderfully patient with me, knowing I was looking at what I could not possibly afford. Sometimes I'd come back twice in a day. He would show me stamps that were beyond my imagination, and well beyond the budget of my fifty-cent allowance. I remember him taking one of his great treasures from his safe for me to see. It was the 1847 Ben Franklin five-cent stamp, the first stamp ever issued by the United States Postal Service, the *Mona Lisa* of philately. Brown tinted, but in remarkably good condition, it was sandwiched in a clear plastic sheath as he placed it in my hands. He clearly knew how important this was to me. He didn't know how insignificant the fifty cents in my pocket felt at that moment. In my little hands I held the oldest and most authentic thing I had ever seen. It was not the last time I saw that tiny, brown stamp. From that time on he showed it to me anytime I asked.

That was not, however, the most authentic moment that my many hobbies had provided me. That distinction belonged to my collection of Indian relics that followed the stamps and preceded the coins. It was a meager gathering of Native American weaponry — arrowheads and grinding stones, mostly. I had never actually found an arrowhead; I bought them one at a time, allowance by allowance, at the Children's Museum of Hartford gift shop. I also became the neighborhood authority on the history of local Indian tribes, the Mohegan, the Pequot, and the Wampanoag who were the early residents on the land on which we lived.

In my exhaustive studies I was surprised to learn that one of the Mohegan tribal villages once stood on the very grounds that were now Indian Hill Cemetery, just down the street from my great-grandmother's home in Middletown, Connecticut. On a Saturday morning visit, my older sister, Carol, and I went there to explore. The grounds were double-hallowed, first from the history of the tribe that once roamed the grassy hills, and then from the eerie silence that now loomed over the resting place for the dead. Many famous state politicians were buried there and we walked among the headstones in awe at the dates that were inscribed, some as far back as 1855. That was really, really old. At the age of nine, centuries and eternity seem interchangeable.

I tell you this story, little William, not only because it is true, but because that day I found something I wasn't looking for. I found something authentic that must have been waiting just for me. I found something that wasn't hidden at all; it was lying in a bed of tall grass, not far from the rows of the famous old headstones. I still remember that one special moment when it caught my eye, and I bent down closer to pick apart the tall grass. There, resting quietly in the grass, in respect, perhaps, for the doubly-hallowed land that had protected it for me for probably one hundred and fifty years or more, was a perfect, blue flint Indian arrowhead.

It was a royal flush–type of moment. My mind wouldn't let me believe the jewel my eyes had discovered. I reached down gently and picked it up as though it were a wounded bird. Then I screamed once it was actually in my hands. My sister came over to witness my discovery. I had never seen an actual arrowhead in its natural habitat, only in the glass case at the Children's Museum Gift Shop. In that irreplaceable moment, I was connected to a Mohegan warrior who, for some intentional and inexplicable reason, had left this precious artifact for me to find many lifetimes later. My mind flooded with questions, all important ones about him, as I struggled to make sense of my new treasure and the message within.

We left the cemetery in a sprint. I had to run back to my great-grandmother's house to show the world my Holy Grail. No one would believe it until I showed them. I gripped it tightly in my hand, not trusting it to my pockets and out of view. I couldn't run fast enough. I ran so fast, in fact, that I didn't look at the stretch of sidewalk in front of me. If I had, I would have noticed one particular slab had shifted up in the corner as a victim of a winter frost-heave. It caught the tip of my toe and I began the same, spinning, slow-motion tumble that I would reenact many years later in my first professional appearance onstage. I was hurtling through the air when my hand let go and I watched one of the last great discoveries on earth fly beyond me — blue flint, end over end — and shatter on the hard concrete. It was all over in an instant.

The damage done was not as great as the damage to my heart. The tip had cracked off and was lost somewhere in the neatly clipped grass along the sidewalk. I searched on my knees for it for an hour. How ironic that an arrowhead that had waited for me for so long, lying so patiently for nearly two centuries, could disappear so quickly in newly mowed grass. I never found the tip of my arrowhead. I walked the rest of the way home, the owner of an authentic story and authentically damaged goods.

The arrowhead is gone today, as are all the hobbies. I have to confess to being as much a capitalist as a romantic. When I finished with each hobby and found another to take its place, I would quietly invite my younger twin brothers, Bruce and Neal, to my room, lock the door, and hold them captive until they acquiesced and bought the old hobby from me. Needless to say, hobbies hold a different meaning for them to this day.

I was too young and too absorbed with what might have been to realize that the real treasure was not an authentic arrowhead; it was the richness of the historical experience, the coincidental connection of a little boy and an Indian warrior. Each of my hobbies brought me stories that have now survived another half century. Perhaps that was the real reason an Indian warrior secretly placed an arrowhead on the ground one hundred and fifty years ago, to give a little boy the memory of an authentic moment. And that is a currency no video game will ever deliver.

If I had to sum it all up, Will, I would say that it is our growing preoccupation with *ease* that has become the natural enemy of the authentic life. Bob Costas pointed it out in our impromptu airborne summit years ago; the loss of authenticity has permeated every aspect of life. I see it perhaps most visibly in the world of entertainment. It is easier to rely less on stories of the human experience in film, and more on spectacles and special effects. We watch people eat worms on television and call it entertainment. We create television contests that mock the genuine process of dating and, even worse, the institution of marriage. We overload ourselves with programming that rewards ambition rather than talent, and then curiously call it "reality" television. The irony is, it is neither real nor authentic. This slow, deliberate loss is, instead, much like the patch of grass in my New York apartment, when what the world really needs is a good long walk.

So, Will, try not to think of Scoshi or me as cynics. We're not. But there is the sound of distant thunder and we both hear it. We are merely voices in the crowd on the route of the Royal Parade shouting that the emperor isn't wearing any clothes. Scoshi lives his life authentically because he is a dog; he has no other choice. But it is precisely because you and I have choices that we can be seduced by the ease of synthetic moments, of moments without meaning. Eventually, though, we will be left abandoned by the gradual emptiness they promise. Warriors have left things in this world for you as well, Will, as they did for me, but you must go out and find them. I do not know what the world below will look like when you are old enough to gaze out the windows of the many planes that will carry you through life. I can only hope that you decide to expect more from life by choosing to live it authentically.

Remember to Put the "U" in Humor

Dear Little Pink Thing,

Dogs don't have regrets. We don't have a lot of expectations, either. But if I had one wish, it would be to laugh. I watch Mom and Dad do it a lot and it looks like fun. But God gave laughter to people, and it looks more and more like you're growing into one of them, so I hope you learn to laugh, too. Watch Dad, he laughs a lot at himself. It's mostly because he does a lot of stupid things.

But don't worry about me, my life is pretty good. I can smell things you can't.

I'm not quite sure how to take his note, but I'm sure there is a compliment tucked in there somewhere.

Every new event in life brings a new opportunity to laugh. That thought was on my mind yesterday morning when little William and I began our morning wrestling match over a new diaper. I was barely awake at 6 a.m., when I put my extra-large coffee mug down on the edge of the changing table and began to undertake the Changing of the Diaper, a ritual that for me and my intuitive abilities seems to take the better part of the day, and that's after I get the hang of it. They're upside down, they're inside out, and you're always trying to hit a moving target. But I made a promise to my wife that since she carried William for nine months, the least I could do is help change his diapers. Be careful of the promises you make.

This particular morning the negotiations were moving along with particular precision. The snaps on his onesie popped open; his legs flipped out effortlessly. With one hand, I picked up both of his chubby little feet to raise him up, slid his pajamas back up under his back, and cleared the playing field. I set him back down as my fingers tore back the adhesive tabs on either side of his diaper. I peeled back the top of the padding and revealed what everyone wants to see along with their morning coffee — a big, poopy diaper. He hadn't just filled the diaper, he had christened it. It was every-where. This set me off my game a bit. I was pretty good with the clear fluids, but this was a job for FEMA.

Will was taking this mess in good spirits, smiling away and making his little squeaking noises as anyone would when finally released from this amount of fecal baggage. Without thinking, I began to operate unconsciously with the training I got from my wife — wrap up the old diaper in a neat little package, put it aside, grab the moistened wipes, and begin to clean up what seemed like two or three square miles of baby mud. I was cleaning and tossing, cleaning and tossing, until I finally began to see the color of infant flesh appearing from beneath the muck. I grabbed the toxic pile of dirty wipes, wrapped them up with the hundred-pound soiled diaper, and dropped the whole mess into the bottomless white bin next to the changing table, where it was effectively removed from the face of the earth.

So far a flawless performance, I thought, the kind where the cattle roper finishes his cattle knot with a snap of his wrist high in the air to the cheers of the crowd. Like a gymnast who'd just stuck his dismount off the parallel bars, I should have arched my back and raised my arms to await the judges' score.

Little William was as good as new. I had forgotten only one thing. One important thing. Actually one fundamental thing. In fact, if you are following along with this process, you probably know the one very, very vital thing that I had forgotten to do.

I neglected to place a tissue over Will's penis to prevent what was happening now before my eyes. As I turned to him to install the brand-new diaper, Will took advantage of the opportunity to pee in a clear, fresh arc straight into my cup of coffee. *Pride goeth before a fall.*

Truly, this new experience of new life has brought new reasons to laugh. I chuckle at all the accoutrements that seem to accompany the raising of an infant. Indeed, we have spent something near a king's ransom buying touchy-feely toys to stimulate his sensory curiosity. We have purchased Baby Einstein videos to encourage him to unlock the baby genius in his mind (hopefully without actually looking like Einstein). Best of all, we have a small audio device that is used each night to lull him to sleep as it hangs on the railing of his crib. It plays a variety of ocean sounds, different patterns of surf, and the sound of seagulls. But it is stuffed into the body of a little sheep. I call it Lamb o' the Sea. I want to know what committee (individuals don't make this broad a blunder) reached the collective conclusion that Greatest Hits of the Ocean should be showcased in the body of a woolly little barnyard animal. I have every reason to believe that someday I will take William by the hand as we walk through the surf at the edge of the shoreline, and he will ask me, "Dad, where are the sheep?"

Even my wife has found a good laugh at the often onerous responsibility of motherhood. When she needs nursing supplies, she drives to a store called, of all things, the Pump Station. In New York City, she visits the Upper Breast Side. (No joke, no joke.)

But nothing makes me laugh harder than William's response to my costume as King Arthur in *Monty Python's Spamalot,* the popular musical spoof of the Knights of the Round Table in which I star in Las Vegas. When in costume, I am covered in gold chain mail from head to toe. I have a crown (all fathers have one, too, I just choose to wear mine) as well as a long broadsword that hangs from my gold, brocaded leather waistband. The look in Will's eyes before he bursts out into laughter makes my heart melt. It's a wide-eyed expression that says, *My dad is my very own action figure.* He tugs and pulls at each piece of the royal costume as I hold him in my arms backstage every evening before beginning each show. The lightness you bring to my heart, William, is unlike any I have ever felt.

Lightness is the purpose of humor. It is God's gift to us that we fight the effects of gravity with levity. It was G. K. Chesterton who said it best: "Angels fly because they take themselves lightly."

I discovered humor early in life because my father loved to laugh — and not just laugh, *ha-ha,* but laugh convulsively. When my father found something funny, and he often did, he would start to squint and then shake his head forward. Then as the laugh grew deeper it would consume him and he would start to shiver and shake. Tears would pour from his eyes. And he wouldn't breathe. And he wouldn't make a sound. My father would laugh without sound or breath. At last, when he reached the point of respiratory failure, his chest would heave back, and his mouth would open slightly and produce this thundering long-drawn sucking sound that stopped everyone in their tracks. When his lungs were sufficiently reloaded, he would start this silent, breathless seizure all over again. I don't know if laughter could ever be a cause of death, but it may very well take my father.

Needless to say, this spectacle was pretty

neat to watch for all of us kids. A couple of well-chosen words to wrap around a good story, a snappy punch line, and we could make our father shake, cry, and drool. It was real power. So all five kids would gather at the dinner table each night not to eat, but to try and make our father laugh.

I regard a sense of humor as the highest form of intelligence, because it demonstrates that you understand not only what is correct with the world, but also what is askew. I have often found the smartest, most well-informed people to be some of the funniest because they have more comedic colors on their palettes from which to choose.

But, William, it is not enough to have a *sense* of humor. Humor must have a "U" or more directly, *you,* in it as well. Ethel Barrymore, an actress and part of the famous Barrymore entertainment tribe, who was as famous for turning down Winston Churchill's proposal for marriage as she was for her film and theatrical career, said, "You grow up the day you have your first real laugh at yourself." She is right. The day I discovered that what I am should be the source of my humor was the most freeing day of my life. The virtue of self-deprecation is the greatest gift that any human being can give to themselves. When we laugh at our expectations in a constantly imperfect world, we numb the disappointments that constantly abound. Laughing at oneself is the best way to deaden the pain of regret. It is also a wonderful defense — laugh at yourself first and no one can take a better shot at you after that.

I'm not sure when it occurred to me that humor is best when it is directed inward. But I suspect the reason I've come to believe this is, as Scoshi says in his note, I do a lot of stupid things. My stupidity might be a little more comic than most because I seem to have such lofty expectations. Consequently I take longer to fall.

I recall auditioning back in the mid-eighties for a musical role that I always wanted to play — Lancelot, the leading man in the musical *Camelot.* It was being staged at the Darien Dinner Theater, about an hour's train ride into Connecticut from Manhattan. I went there on a late Saturday morning to audition for the role along with dozens of other hopefuls. I prepared the material carefully, a couple of scenes from the script and music from Lancelot's famous romantic ballad, "How to Handle a Woman." I also dressed my best. I selected a nice blue shirt, with a few too many buttons open at the chest. I complemented the very trendy ensemble with a pair of crisp white cotton slacks and poufy hair (compliments of my portable hair dryer that I used without regard for human life). I was the perfect kit-specimen of a mid-eighties Broadway leading man.

The train arrived uncharacteristically early in Darien that warm spring morning, so it was an easy walk to the theater, and I had plenty of time to prepare before the audition. I went over the scenes in my head and hummed my way through the lyrics to the song. Finally, the casting director came up to me and told me that I was on deck to go into the theater for my audition. I thought I would use the last few moments to freshen up my appearance in the men's room. Inside the bathroom, I primped a bit by the mirror, practiced my song with the pleasant enhancement of the echo off the bathroom tile, and wished myself good luck. Then I looked down at my pants. All the time that I had been standing and giving my performance to the men's room mirror, I didn't realize that I had been standing so close to the counter that my crisp white cotton slacks were absorbing the entire puddle of water that was left around the sink. Not a few harmless drops, but enough water to wash a Buick with. And when white cotton pants absorb enough water they reach a saturation point and become transparent, and on me they revealed my Speedo-cut black underwear that was also a necessary part of the mid-eighties wardrobe. At that point, the men's room door opened a crack and the female casting director announced through the crack that they were ready for me. I was flush with panic. Where was my automatic hair dryer now, when I really needed one? I was completely surrounded by diaphanousness — flimsy paper towels and translucent toilet paper. It would be hours before I was dry. I was hopelessly marinated.

I didn't get the role as Lancelot. It went to someone else. I offered no explanation to the faceless few in the darkened theater who were present for my audition that morning. I sang well, I read well, and I looked right, but damp. I have to believe that when they made their casting choice for a leading man my apparent incontinence must have weighed heavily on their minds.

I enjoy reprising that story as much as I enjoy having been the subject of it. I have arrived at the point in my life where I enjoy laughing at it as much as I enjoy living it.

William, I think what Scoshi was trying to

tell you in his letter was that you are lucky enough to be born into a funny home. Not a home for jokes, but a normal place with normal things with normal people who find the humor in being normal. I hope you are comfortable with that.

I hope you are comfortable with the idea that in this family humor must be about us before it can be about others. G. K. Chesterton also wrote, "It is the test of a good religion if you can tell a joke about it." I have no doubt in my mind he was also measuring a good person's character by how well he could take a joke.

After all, my little boy, we are all bozos on the bus, and never forget that. We are only blood and tissue. Some days it all lines up correctly and some days it doesn't. When it doesn't, we have God. But when He is silent, He gives us dogs and laughter.

ON WATCHES AND WALLETS: HOW TO SPEND TIME AND MONEY

Dear Little Pink Thing,

I don't know much about time. I know what now means, and I know what never means. Because I know the meaning of now, I can nap when I'm tired and eat when I'm hungry. I can bark when I'm happy and bark when I'm not. But I don't have too many plans or fears and I don't know what regret is. I'm pretty content with all this. But time seems to be important to Dad, so it'll probably be important to you, too. He always says he doesn't have enough of it.

I don't know much about money, either; I am pretty free without it. But that also seems to be important to Dad. He says he doesn't have enough of that, either. So if you ever find some extra time or money, please give it to him. I think he'll appreciate it.

This letter made me laugh out loud. I never realized Scoshi to be so beneficent and concerned about my material well-being. But he wrote the note to underscore the importance that time and money will play in your life, Will. And believe it or not, despite his statement to the contrary, he is more of an expert than he admits.

Time and money, Will, are inextricably attached. You will find this out very soon when you learn to tell time and to count your pennies. The world is both a clock and a piggy bank. Time and money are the common measures of human experience. You cannot conceive of an activity that takes place outside of time, and, just as true, you cannot imagine a human action that is free from expense.

Scoshi was quick to point out that he has limited experience with time and money and that is simply because he is a dog. The awareness of time and the need for money are distinctly human experiences. But because they are human experiences, and important ones, our attitudes about time and money can be the cause of joy or misery, a source of balance and prosperity, or the basis for fear and stress. How we handle time and money will in large part determine the quality of our lives.

■ ■ ■ ■

I have been fascinated by the concept of time since I was a youngster and was first told about the idea of eternity as part of my early Catholic education. Eternity, we were told, meant forever and ever and always was. I would have a mental meltdown every time I tried to conceive of what eternity meant. Kind of like the brain freeze you get from overdoing a spoonful of ice cream. But eternity also struck me as kind of a lonely concept. God must have had no friends for a long, long time, and had to keep Himself busy by creating things and eventually people. I wasn't sure how much company we were for God, especially given some of the behavior of my classmates. But I always assumed God knew what He was doing.

I realized early on, though, that we are surrounded by time. It is everywhere. We are greeted by sunup, then sundown. Even our language is constructed to explain our actions within the context of time. Verbs are conjugated in terms of past, present, and future. We develop our expectations of time early, and are quick to plan what we want to be when we grow up. Our age becomes so important that we chop up a year into fractions when asked how old we are. We try to stay up late at night because time in later hours of the evening is the laurels of adulthood. And, of course, strapped to our little wrists are ways to record time by the whereabouts of a big hand and a little hand.

But time loses both its fascination and its innocence as we grow older and develop responsibilities. Work must be accomplished within finite amounts of time, bills have due dates, we buy time for quarters at parking meters, our lives are measured in miles per hour, and we make promises to others "till death do us part." Time becomes a burden as we feel ourselves age. As Scoshi pointed out so personally, I never seem to have enough of it. We live privately in fear of the moment that we will eventually run out of it.

So, my son, I would like to share with you three suggestions that, for me, comprise a healthy notion of time — a personal one, which I have made my own. I offer them to you as a way to embrace the concept of time so that it will embellish your life and not degrade it by becoming a source of fear or stress. All come from experience, and believe it or not, from the dog who sleeps so faithfully at the foot of your chair.

■ ■ ■ ■

Live in the present moment. I learned this from Scoshi. When he describes how free he is to live spontaneously — napping and eating at will, and so on, he does so because for him time is no burden. He has no concept of what he has to accomplish nor what he failed to do. No past and no future. He experiences life from moment to moment. He looks you directly in the eye and absorbs everything that is there without the worry that he might be missing a better conversation. To a dog, every moment is full of meaning.

I learned a bit about the idea of the present moment in my formal training as an actor. I have sat through endless successions of seemingly cryptic exercises, staring into the eyes of another actor, free-associating feelings, dealing only with what is presently available to me. As meaningless as they seem, these exercises train you to become aware of the present moment. Indeed, the best actors are those who have learned to respond honestly to what is happening in the here and now. It is what makes acting the art of the infinite possibility.

But it is misleading to think that we can

live *literally* in the present. Time is constantly fluid, moving through us like a river. A moment passes as quickly as it is perceived. So let me give you a practical example of what, to me, it means to live in the present moment.

One morning, over a cup of coffee, still foggy from sleep, I was sitting in our family room without any of the usual distractions. Your mother had just left the house and was headed to the airport with you to visit your grandparents in Colorado. (I didn't go because I had a show that night.) The house was empty and strangely quiet, Will, for the first time since you were born. The dogs were midway through their morning naps, and I was gently rocking in the feeding chair, noticing that the wonderful energy from your mother and you was sadly absent.

I continued staring and contemplating until I was suddenly aware of what I was staring at. It was the corner of the room of the rented house that we were living in temporarily in Las Vegas. It was spectacularly uninteresting, but I was staring at it as a way of giving my eyes something to do while my mind was busy missing my family. Gradually, though, I became aware that I was staring at the junction of two stucco walls, a small green plant, and a couple of oak TV trays that for some reason had made a home there. Clearly not the stuff to inspire great thought, but apparently perfectly adequate for my level of comprehension. I began to move the focus of my thinking to this bland little corner. I started thinking about the TV trays. I looked at the surfaces of each, how they had been planed smooth, but how beautifully the grain of the wood made a unique pattern on each. It occurred to me that there were no two wooden TV trays alike anywhere, like there are no two identical snowflakes. Each had the individual stamp of God's design in nature. I then thought about the person who planed them smooth. I was imagining him being from China. I began to wonder about the life of a person who had such a job. What did he aspire to? What was the day like for him when he completed these two trays? Did he have a family? Did he care for them as deeply as I did mine? I thought, too, that he most assuredly never knew when he assembled these two trays that someday, thousands of miles away, halfway across the globe, it would cause another human being to pause long enough to admire his work and to think kindly of him.

My eyes shifted to the plant, which sat dutifully yet incongruously below the TV trays in a natural wicker pot on the floor. I'm sure if it could execute a choice, it would not be where it is — in a nondescript stucco corner of a stucco home in the stucco neighborhoods of Las Vegas. But there it was, a quiet sentinel keeping watch on some forsaken post. It was silently serving its only purpose within God's Great Plan, exchanging the air we breathe. I then thought about that Plan, its intricate design of interdependency. The plant takes care of me as long as I give it light and water, which I don't. But apparently someone does; it is green and healthy. It is not the first time someone else has had to pick up the slack for me in the natural order of things.

But I quietly reflect on the fact that the Great Plan extends beyond me and beyond the plant. It extends to the tiny cellular and atomic structures that are the essence of us both. It is as large as the celestial bodies that spin and circle through the heavens and obey the physical laws that hold us all in place. The more I reflect on God's Great Plan, the more I am humbled and filled with awe. I also get the same brain freeze that I got as a kid trying to contemplate eternity.

All of this was contained in a few present moments that would have otherwise passed by without significance. And yet, whether or not we pause to acknowledge it, the meaning is always there. Will, there are many corners like this in the world. The more you use a present moment to observe them and not ignore them, the more your life will feel connected to a deeper sense of purpose, the more you will sense the Great Plan that is happening all around you, all the time, and the more you will appreciate that you have a place in it.

Never presuppose a worry. Fear is the worst way to spend time. When we are afraid, we have empowered our imagination with the notion that we cannot handle what comes our way. This notion is simply and categorically wrong. We have been given by God the ability to cope with all things, *all things,* even the moment of death.

A sense of worry is always about a future event, and while you are absorbed by worry you can think of nothing but the future. But it comes at the expense of everything else that is good and meaningful, because while you are busy worrying, countless moments will pass you by, and with them go a million chances to truly experience something infinitely more real than the source of your worry.

I lived with worry every day of my early

life as an actor. It took the form of stage fright. It crippled my enjoyment of what I had felt all my life so driven to do. Stage fright is the worst thing that an actor can develop. It starts early in the afternoon before the evening performance. There is tension in the body. You feel uncomfortable in your skin. There is a growing knot in your stomach. Your hands melt with sweat. Your mind begins to race and you become filled with self-doubt. *What will happen if I'm really no good and no one has had the courage to tell me? It worked last night, but what happens if I can't generate the same performance tonight? Will I be able to hit the high note? What if I forget my lines?* And on and on.

What is strange about stage fright is that, for most people, it disappears the moment the stage lights go up. Somehow in the adrenaline rush of public performance, the paralyzing tension of self-doubt evaporates. The focus you give your character takes over, and the instincts that made you great the night before and on other stages and on other nights consume and guide you through the performance.

So did I have grounds for my fear? No, of course not. I had simply decided to become absorbed in the uncertain future and bless it with doubt, rather than enjoy the present moment and bless it with the excitement of having a chance to once again fulfill my lifelong wish to be an actor. During those years, I continually missed the chance at a million wonderful moments by worrying about what was uncertain.

This changed early one evening on a bus to New Jersey, a perfect place for this type of epiphany. I was heading out to the New Jersey Shakespeare Festival in Madison for opening night. I was going to be performing one of the roles in the two-man comedy *Mass Appeal.* It was my third year in New York, the fall of 1984. This play and the role were a benchmark for me, as it was for most young actors like myself in New York. It was a coming-of-age play about a young seminarian and an elderly parish priest and their clash of ideals. This role was my Hamlet, it was a role I felt born to perform because of my sensitivity to the material and the message of the play.

And yet, all of the meaning was missing on the bus ride that evening from Manhattan to the theater. In its place were a single knot and a flock of butterflies in my stomach, lots of sweat, and a mind spinning with panic. I was sitting in the back of the bus by myself gazing out the window at who knows what — probably a corner of the world that

I was incapable of seeing. It was opening night and I was too busy being subdued by worry to appreciate the moment.

Somewhere during the hour's ride, however, and I can't tell you where or why, something changed. I recall being angry at myself for my fear and my inability to enjoy this cornerstone moment. But that's when I told myself to stop. I told myself that I had come too far, trained too hard, and given up too much to not believe in myself. It was then that I realized that I was capable of handling anything that happened — even a bad review, which for an actor is worse than the moment of death. I continued to talk to myself right up to the instant that the curtain rose on that opening night.

What I remember about *Mass Appeal* was not the quality of my performance (I was spectacular) but that I broke the back of the crippling effects of worry. To this day I never have so much as a nervous twitch before I go onstage. My mind is filled with only one promise — that whatever happens, I will have the time of my life. And I always do.

Live your life backward. You can manage the quality of your time in this life much better when you know where you are going. And the best way to know where you are going is to decide where you want to end up. That is what I mean by living your life backward.

This may sound like simple fluff, but I mean this deeply, Will: Asking yourself fundamental questions about what you imagine to be the punctuation point of your life will tell you a lot about how you should complete the sentence.

I asked myself fundamental questions back in my twenties, when I made the commitment to leave public relations and refocus and reinvigorate my desire to be an actor. I simply couldn't imagine the disappointment I would feel having left this world as anything but an actor. When all was said and done, that was how I wanted to have defined myself. Consequently, I started doing all the things that I needed to do to prepare for that journey. Even though I was filled with doubts, I knew that if I was successful in defining my journey, I would be successful in my attempt to get there.

These important questions should have fluid responses, because your life is constantly changing. The answers should never be intractable. When I met your mother I decided that I no longer wanted to define myself by my bachelorhood, so I changed the direction of my life. This was the second time I posed the question of how I wanted my life to end. I decided that I wanted to leave this world embracing her as deeply as I could hug and remembering how much we loved each other. So I do everything I can to provide the healthiest environment to make sure that that time, God willing, is a long way off. I work out. I take care of my body and my mind to delay the inevitable entropy, and because of that I am a healthier, more vibrant being than I was without her. When you finally came into our lives, William, my answers changed yet again, along with our decisions on where and how we live. What did not change was that in my imagination, my final moment will be an embrace that will be big enough and deep enough for you both.

But just as every action is defined by time, all human activity also has a cost, and that cost is most often measured in money. And just as our attitude about time will determine how we enjoy it, our attitude about money will do the same.

Let's begin by defining our terms. Money is freedom, Will. It is as simple as that. The more money you have, the more you are able to do what you *choose* to do versus what you *have* to do.

Your attitude about money is a much more complex discussion. If you regard money as a finite thing that will be limited in its availability to you, then you will hoard it. You will reduce the number of opportunities that life will offer you so as not to strain the available supply. Your life will also reflect the elements of the rainy day that you have so diligently saved for.

If you have a disregard for the importance of money by spending it frivolously on fleeting pleasures with no intrinsic or lasting value, then you will live desperately, from one "fix" of money to the next.

If, however, you regard money as an instrument of prosperity your life will take on a different quality. Money will not be finite, but will come into your life and be dispensed as necessary to live an extraordinary life. You will spend, not with reluctance or fear, but with a sense of freedom and excitement over the value of what you pursue and the joy it brings. You will spend it on yourself and your loved ones because it brings you pleasure. You will spend freely on what has a deeper value, knowing that you have the ability to replace money with more money.

You will invest in yourself. A prosperous person knows that every dollar reinvested in their ability to earn provides returns that are geometric to their cost. You will invest outside yourself in responsible vehicles. Your respect for value will force you to avoid gambling, lotteries, and get-rich-quick promises as a means to affluence. You will budget your money wisely because you will respect sound economic principles.

You will also learn to give without promise of return. You will be generous to the degree you can because you realize that the blessing of prosperity carries with it an obligation to leave the world around you better than how you found it.

But a caution here. Being prosperous does not necessarily mean being rich. It means balancing your wealth with your needs. You determine the quality and freedom necessary to keep you happy and set your income to reflect that.

Some of the freest and most prosperous times I've experienced also were times when I had very little money. My first summer after college, when I worked as a singing waiter (the one where I fell flat on my face opening night), I earned roughly a hundred dollars a week from salary and tips. I shared an off-campus apartment that rented during summer months for forty-five dollars a month. (My roommate was the captain of the college basketball team and spent the summer preparing for a tryout with an NBA team. He had many supporters of his noble effort, including grocers and butchers in the area who wanted to make sure that he, and consequently I, was well fed.) I had a bike to ride to the theater and a girlfriend with a car. If I wanted to take her to dinner on my night off, I had enough money. I went to the beach during the day and got to pursue my theatrical passion by night. It was the first time I had felt the freedom that comes from having enough money to fit your standard of living. I felt prosperous on a hundred dollars a week. I still feel that way today. It's just the numbers that have changed.

I encourage you, too, Will, to adopt a prosperous attitude toward money. That way you will control it rather than the other way around, and you avoid both economic and spiritual poverty.

Somehow I know these words will come back to haunt me when it comes time to negotiate your allowance.

EPILOGUE

Dear William,

That's what everyone seems to call you now, so I begin my last letter by calling you that, too. You haven't grown nearly enough fur, so I no longer believe that you will become a dog. I am disappointed, but I can understand that you want to be like Mom and Dad. Well, Mom, anyway. I'm still not sure Dad is the best of his breed.

I hope you get my notes. I am leaving them here under the foot of the Big Blue Elephant. Someday you will find them when you get curious about why he sits there so still.

My letters will tell you what to do so that he, and other Big Blue Elephants, cannot harm you. They will try to get you to do things that aren't good for you. Big Blue Elephants are blue because they are unhappy with themselves. But

Big Blue Elephants are most afraid of real men.

They blame others for things they should have done. They do not keep their word, and they always take the easy road home. Big Blue Elephants almost never do anything authentic. They waste your time and your money. They cannot take a joke, but will always laugh at the fate of others. They are attractive to look at, but they don't regard the heart as a precious thing. And at their heart, they are very much alone.

Even more curiously, Dad and I have never seen a Big Blue Elephant fishing.

No Big Blue Elephants will hurt you as long as I am around. But I will not be here much longer. I can't see very well anymore. I cannot hear you, although I suspect you laugh when you wave your hands and smile like you do. My legs don't work like they used to, so Dad has to carry me a lot.

I do not know where I am going, William, but I think that someday I will wake up and I will stop being a dog. I am not scared. I think it is something that will just happen. I just hope that wherever I go, I am fed well and loved as much as Dad and Mom have loved me. Well, Mom, anyway. Dad always messed up my meals.

Wherever I go, though, always remember that I will be watching, and I will always be there for you. I made that promise to you the first night I sat in front of the Big Blue Elephant. And real men always keep their promises.

Your dog,
Scoshi

It took a while for me to read this note to you, Will, because it hurt too much when I discovered it. It is sad to be reminded that all the wonderful things of this world, especially my relationship with Scoshi, are not blessed with permanence. As authentic as they may be, they are temporary.

So I saved it to read in the most authentic place at the most authentic time I could think of. Together, not long ago, we sat one evening at sunset on the edge of a high, tall grass bluff overlooking the ocean on the south shore of the island of Nantucket. It is authentic because Nantucket is a place where time is as important as it is unimportant. They have protected and preserved the presence of the eighteenth century, and have protected the land so that private, present moments are still possible on ocean bluffs like the one where you and I sat. It is also a place where flags still fly in front of most homes. There was just enough breeze coming off the water that evening to make the flags furl and to make us both squint, which hid my tears as I read you the note.

It was the first time you had seen the sea and the shore. I watched the wonderment in your eyes, which grew larger than I had ever seen them as you tried to understand the significance of what you saw. You had heard the ocean sounds before from the Lamb o' the Sea. But these were authentic ones. The Lamb o' the Sea was just a patch of grass in a big city apartment. This was the real sand between your toes for the first time, and you were sharing it with your father. You were too young to remember this, but I will.

It was also the same water that crashed to shore on another coast many years ago as I tossed Scoshi a Frisbee that he would not retrieve and fished with calamari that he was only too happy to eat. So it is no coincidence that I was sitting there reading this note, written by the little dog that I treated as my son, while I was holding the real thing.

Will cannot understand you yet, Scoshi, as

you cannot hear him, and he cannot read. But I will make this promise to you — I will take your place in front of the Big Blue Elephant, and I will defend this little boy with my life. I will make sure that his life's homework is always done and that he will be a man of his word.

It is the least I can do for you, since you spent your life fishing with me.

ABOUT THE AUTHOR

Award-winning actor, host, composer, and writer — and lifelong dog lover — **John O'Hurley** is one of television's busiest and most versatile personalities. Since 2002, he has served as the host of NBC's *The National Dog Show presented by Purina®*. In 2005, he danced his way into the hearts of America as the ultimate champion of the hit ABC show *Dancing with the Stars* — and was selected as one of *People* magazine's "sexiest men alive." He is well-known for his portrayal of the wry and witty J. Peterman on *Seinfeld,* and as the voice of popular cartoon characters, such as King Neptune in *SpongeBob SquarePants.* He currently hosts the widely syndicated game show classic *Family Feud.*

In 2006, he made his Broadway debut in the lead male role of Billy Flynn in *Chicago,* and in 2007, he joined the Las Vegas cast of *Monty Python's Spamalot,* as King Arthur.

His first CD, *Peace of Our Minds,* featuring his original piano compositions, also topped the classical charts in 2006. His first book, *It's Okay to Miss the Bed on the First Jump,* was a *New York Times* bestseller.

When he's not performing or writing, John maintains his single-digit handicap by playing on the Celebrity Players Tour and other charity tournaments. He lives in Los Angeles with his wife, Lisa; his son, William; and their two dogs, Betty and Scoshi.

9/08

only